# PARTNERS ON THE PAYROLL

We don't have "hired hands" any more. Bill has helped everyone at One Week Bath think like partners.

—Matt Plaskoff, *President and CEO, One Week Bath*

I love this book! It leads and teaches everything I believe in and have tried to do for the last 20-plus years. In that time we have grown from $7.5 million (which it took 20 years to get to) to over $125 million this year! I know it works and so does every one of my partners! Thanks, Bill!

—Robert Griggs, *Founder and President, Trinity Products*

I read it straight through. What incredible experiences Bill has had coaching companies to build extraordinary success! The feeling of coaching our team and witnessing employees transforming into business partners will stay with me for a long time. Having led a company this way it feels completely foreign to try any other way. Why would you keep employees in the dark? Why would you try to shoulder the burden of solving business problems all to yourself?

—Melissa Hamilton, *Board member and former CEO, Stellar*

The pandemic brought unique challenges to healthcare providers like us. Using this approach allowed us to make dramatic strides in profitability and overall patient care. But culture and employee engagement have always been important, too, and the approach reinforces important cultural aspects like economic engagement, transparency, and teamwork.

—Guru Sankar, *Managing Partner AFC, Urgent Care Portland*

A wonderfully readable book that will help every company owner and manager get the most from their teams. It shows how companies should run—with people, principles and profits.

—Ronald Saks, *President and CEO, LMI Aerospace*

Helping every associate understand how they contribute to the organization's success is key, and we were able to accomplish that in Productions Services at Capital One. Partners on the Payroll wonderfully illustrates the value of all employees acting as committed and engaged owners.

—Dan Mortensen, *President and CEO, Virginia Council on Economic Education*
*Former executive, Capital One*

We have nothing but partners on our payroll at Comfort Supply. Everyone's an owner, and everyone understands the business. I recommend this book to every entrepreneur.

—Clay Blevins, *President and CEO, Comfort Supply*

We worked with Bill Fotsch for many years and he was instrumental in helping us implement open-book management. This management practice elevates employee engagement and creates true partners that work together for the greater good.

—Elizabeth Wilder, *President and CEO, Anthony Wilder Design/Build*

Our company experienced serious challenges following the global financial crisis, and Bill Fotsch helped us navigate them. Today we're a stronger business thanks to the ideas Bill outlines in this book.

—David J. Pring, *CEO, Post Form Laminating*

Bill helped our company operate more profitably by engaging everyone in the economics of the business. This book will show you how to do it.

—Angus Beasley, *Cofounder, Adams + Beasley Associates*

You'll want to buy a copy of this book for everyone on your team, and then put its ideas into action. Quite simply, it's a better way to run a company.

—Janet Wheatley, *Vice President, Traveler Services North and Latin America*
*Carlson Wagonlit Travel (retired)*

Through working with Bill I was able to participate in the process of bringing company and employee goals to the table, resulting in the parties working together instead of at cross purposes. Bill's work made a big difference.

—Warren Johncock, *Union Delegate*

An extremely helpful book. It's the way we run our company.

—Richard Feuerborn, *CFO and Principal Engineer*
*FA Engineering*

# PARTNERS

## ON THE

# PAYROLL

INDIGORIVER
PUBLISHING

# PARTNERS
## ON THE
# PAYROLL

*Improve Your Company's Results.*
*Improve the Lives of the People Who Produce Those Results.*

## BILL FOTSCH
### WITH JOHN CASE

*Partners on the Payroll: Improve Your Company's Results; Improve the Lives of the People Who Produce Those Results*

© 2022 by Bill Fotsch

Indigo River Publishing
3 West Garden Street, Ste. 718
Pensacola, FL 32502
www.indigoriverpublishing.com

Cover and interior design by Emma Grace

Ordering Information:
Quantity sales: Special discounts are available on quantity purchases by corporations, associations, and others. For details, contact the publisher at the address above.
Orders by US trade bookstores and wholesalers: Please contact the publisher at the address above.

Printed in the United States of America

Library of Congress Control Number: 2021911215
ISBN: 978-1-954676-11-4
First Edition

*With Indigo River Publishing, you can always expect great books, strong voices, and meaningful messages.*
*Most importantly, you'll always find . . . words worth reading.*

*I dedicate this book, first and foremost, to my immediate family, who taught and reinforce the basic principles on which this book is based. And to all the partners in my career who embraced treating everyone they encountered as part of their extended family.*

# CONTENTS

# PREFACE

**IMAGINE A COMPANY** where everyone on the payroll is engaged and committed. Where employees are considered trusted partners rather than hired hands. Where everyone has a chance to learn about the business, to contribute to its success, and to share in the wealth they help create.

Such a company would likely be highly profitable—a leader in its market. It would attract and keep the best people. It would be innovative, because employees would regularly come up with new ideas to boost efficiency or better serve customers. It would be an organization that everyone, from the CEO to the accounts-payable clerk, could take pride in being a part of.

As we continue to rebuild the American economy after the coronavirus pandemic, this is the kind of company we need. We need businesses that can compete with anyone in the world. We need businesses that provide all their employees with good jobs, with opportunities to grow, and with a chance to accumulate wealth. We need a system that gives millions of hard-working citizens a chance for a better life, funded by companies that are profitable and growing.

Such a system might be called *partnership capitalism*. The companies that make it up might be called *partnership companies*. They have partners on the payroll, not hired hands.

We may have to wait awhile for the system to develop. But there are plenty of partnership companies around. This book will tell some of their stories. And it will show you how to create one.

# *Introduction*

## THE CLOSET CAPITALIST

**I ARRIVED IN AUSTRALIA** on a Tuesday. I had worked in Europe for a few years early in my career, but I wasn't what you'd call a world traveler. So Australia was a surprise. I had left the US in the middle of winter; now, suddenly, it was summer, hot and dry. The grass was green, the flowers in bloom.

I was there to work with BHP Billiton, known today as just BHP. It's a big mining company with operations all over the world. BHP had a nine-thousand-employee iron ore facility in Port Hedland, on the country's northwest coast. Port Hedland is nearly a thousand miles from Perth, and Perth itself is on the other side of the continent from cities like Sydney and Canberra. I had to take a couple more flights to get to my destination.

Before I arrived, my colleagues and I had conducted a survey of the managers and employees at BHP's facility. We were worried. Management mistrusted labor. Labor hated management. The two groups were often openly hostile. The company's most recent managerial initiative was from the human resources office's so-called Blue Group. It advised the miners to be nicer to each other and to stop swearing. The reaction among the employees was predictable; it showed up in the surveys plain as day. My BHP contacts were hoping I could help them overcome the mistrust and hostility.

We began by conducting ninety-minute sessions for thirty to forty employees at a time. We shared what we learned from the surveys. We showed a video of a company where managers and employees were more like partners. We discussed how we could apply the lessons at BHP. We held twenty sessions that first week.

In the second week, we asked BHP's local managers to provide introductions. One of those introductions still makes me cringe so much that I remember exactly when it happened: Tuesday, the third session of the week. The manager was young. He meant well. But here's what he said: "Bill Fotsch is an internationally recognized management leader, speaker, and consultant. He has worked with companies like Southwest Airlines, Harley-Davidson, Capital One, and the Zambia Consolidated Copper Mine. He graduated top of his class from Harvard Business School. We are fortunate to have him with us."

Eyes were rolling all over the room. I could almost hear the miners thinking, Wow, gee, this guy must be really *special*. So when I got up to speak I tried a different tack. "Thanks for the introduction," I said, "but I think I should set the record straight. I am a Yank. More than that, I'm the worst kind of Yank—a capitalist Yank."

From the back of the room, one of the miners stood up and said, "Well, I'm a socialist."

"Great," I said. "My name is Bill. What's yours?" He told me it was Warren. I encouraged everyone to speak up just the way Warren had. Afterward, I said, we'd see whether a socialist and a capitalist had anything in common.

We went through the survey results and the video of the more progressive company, discussing both along the way. We talked about the implications for BHP's operations in Port Hedland. When the conversation paused, I thanked everyone for contributing and said that it was now time for Warren and me to speak.

I found his face in the crowd and addressed him directly. "Warren, it seems like the miners think they know a lot of different ways to improve the operations around here. Do you think that's right?"

Warren folded his arms across his chest. "Damn right they do."

"Great," I said. "I do too. Seems like a socialist and a capitalist do have things they can agree on. And do you think that management would be wise to do less talking and more listening to the miners' ideas?"

Warren nodded. "You bet they should. It would improve production and morale."

I grinned. "Another thing a capitalist and a socialist agree on. One more question: Do you think BHP would make more money if they listened and acted on the ideas from the troops?"

Warren didn't hesitate. "They would make a hell of a lot more money."

I turned to the forty others in the audience and said, "You heard it from his own lips. Warren is a capitalist. And he is the worst kind of capitalist. He's a *closet* capitalist." The room erupted in laughter, with Warren joining in.

## WHAT'S WRONG WITH CAPITALISM?

The Australian trip took place more than a decade ago. I was a capitalist then and I'm a capitalist now. I believe it's a great economic system. It allows a high degree of individual freedom. It encourages entrepreneurship, risk taking, and competition, all of which are critical to economic growth and a better standard of living. The developed nations of the world—in North America, western Europe, parts of Asia—owe their high standards of living to capitalism. Even China's communist leaders discovered the virtues of capitalism a few decades back and began to open up the nation's economy. China is still fuzzy on the individual freedom part, but its economic performance has been the envy of the world. Over the past thirty years it has lifted millions of people out of grinding dollar-a-day poverty and given them an opportunity for a better life.

So what's wrong with capitalism? People have written countless books about this question. But from my perspective there's one big problem: capitalism creates two groups of people.

One group gets it. They understand how business creates wealth. Many of these people are company owners, executives, or investors. Some may be in government or the professions, but they are generally supportive of business. By "generally," of course, I don't mean "blindly." Business, like every other human endeavor, has its share of bad apples who have to be reined in. But those who understand how business works appreciate the value of the system as a whole. And they typically do pretty well by it.

The other group doesn't get it, and in most cases it's through no fault of their own. They weren't taught much about how business works in school. They come from neighborhoods where most people are on someone else's payroll, if they have jobs at all. Their approach to making a living is to find the best job available and hope it lasts. To this group, business can seem like a scam and *profit* like a dirty word. They believe that the hallmark of business is exploitation. Some think that a socialist system, however defined, would be preferable.

Most companies, unfortunately—even companies that aspire to offer great workplaces—don't do much to change those beliefs. They pay their employees a wage or a salary, period. They tell those employees what to do. The companies never explain the economics of the business—in fact, they typically make a point of keeping their financial strategies and business results secret from the people on the front line. (Even publicly traded companies, which have to release their consolidated financials, rarely share the performance of individual branches or business units with their workers.) Most companies, moreover, don't give workers much of a chance to think for themselves and take responsibility. Of course, what would be the point? If the employees don't understand the economics of the business, they'd be unlikely to make good decisions anyway.

So employees, for the most part, come to think and act like hired hands: "Just tell me what to do and I'll do it." They focus on doing their jobs. If they have ideas, they keep those ideas to themselves. Many aren't very happy or engaged in their work—and indeed, why would they be? Nobody asks their opinion; nobody trusts them with important information.

This is a situation that can easily generate mistrust and resentment, just as it did at BHP. Employees come to believe that management doesn't care about them or what they think (often quite true). Management comes to believe that employees have to be closely supervised or they'll never get anything done (also often true). Money, of course, is always a bone of contention and a source of mistrust. Employees probably don't know how much money the company is making, but they do know that they see only a tiny piece of it. So they figure that the boss and the owners must be getting rich (often the case). For their part, owners and managers frequently feel that the company would be more profitable if only they could cut labor costs. The siren song of layoffs always beckons, and employees know that they are always vulnerable. Layoffs, which decades ago were associated with business downturns and inept management, are now often greeted with an increase in the stock price.

Once upon a time, capitalism's two groups fought out their differences on the picket line and at the ballot box. In 1920—more than a century ago—the US experienced 3,400 strikes.[1] Many of them were both bitter and bloody. Many were led by avowed socialists. My own great-grandfather worked as a machinist in Milwaukee, making metal parts with lathes, drills, and other equipment. It was a skilled job. But he saw companies taking actions that he felt were not in the best interests of his fellow workers or his family, so he helped develop the machinists' union in the city.* Union organizing, in turn, contributed to the pro-labor socialist movement, especially in the Midwest. Eugene V. Debs, the Socialist Party's candidate for president, got nearly a million votes in the 1920 election. More than seventy thousand of them came from Milwaukee.[2]

Today we rarely see the same level of open animosity between labor and management. Unions have been on the decline for decades. (My great-grandfather left the very union he helped create, as he saw it becoming corrupt and ineffective.) Nor do we see much in the way of socialism, despite the rhetoric of Bernie Sanders and his allies. But no one should make the mistake of assuming that everything is hunky-dory with American capitalism, either inside or outside the walls of US business. Consider these facts:

In 2000, the Gallup organization found that fewer than 30 percent of US workers reported themselves engaged in their work. By 2019, the

---

* My great-grandfather's son—my grandfather—was quite different. Pop, as he was known in the family, set up his own business, selling machine tools for companies like Kearney & Trecker. He held two patents. He sat on the board of one of his customers. His was a classic American success story, complete with leaving school in the fifth grade to work and make money for the family. The arguments between union member/socialist father and capitalist son were fierce. Looking back, I see the good in both of them. I think they were both right.

number had ticked up to 35 percent, no doubt the result of an extraordinarily tight labor market. Still, about two-thirds of American employees remain not engaged (and in fact, Gallup's number dropped in mid-2020 to 31 percent, probably because of the pandemic).[3]

Polls consistently show that between 50 and 80 percent of workers are actively looking for a new job. Gallup says that the 65 percent of employees who are either "actively disengaged" or "not engaged" are "on the lookout for better employment opportunities and will quickly leave their company for a slightly better offer."[4] If you run a typical company, in other words, about two-thirds of your workers are probably dreaming about working somewhere else.

From 1973 to 2018, inflation-adjusted wages for ordinary workers were essentially flat.[5] Meanwhile, a dollar's worth of stock grew (in real terms) to $14.10.[6] So people who work for a living have seen their incomes stagnate, while people with significant income from capital ownership have done very well. That's a sure-fire recipe for frustration and resentment.

Typically, the highest level of engagement for most employees is when they are first hired. Engagement then falls as the years go on—quite a condemnation of most companies' management.

Many people still live paycheck to paycheck and so are plagued by insecurity. A Federal Reserve survey in 2018 found that four in ten US adults would have trouble coming up with $400 in an emergency.[7] About half of Americans fifty-five and older have no retirement savings.[8]

Most of these statistics, of course, were compiled before the coronavirus pandemic, and thus before the raft of economic difficulties that it led to. At this writing, the economy seems to be recovering. Still, millions of people have lost their jobs.

But even before the virus, attitudes weren't exactly favorable to capitalism. "Recent polls suggest a substantial majority of Americans feel the economy is working only for those in power," wrote Yale political scientist Jacob Hacker in 2019.[9] Many young people, burdened by student debt and facing uncertain prospects in the labor market, pronounced themselves disaffected with the whole system. In one widely reported poll, Americans age eighteen to twenty-nine viewed socialism more positively than capitalism.[10] Some business leaders were worrying that such attitudes would spread. "Capitalists Fear a Socialist Revolt" was the headline for a 2019 *New York Times* article that stated, "Ray Dalio of Bridgewater Associates and Jamie Dimon of JPMorgan Chase have both recently said they believed capitalism needs to be reformed if it is to survive."[11]

## REFORMING CAPITALISM

To me, the reform of capitalism begins with business. Entrepreneurs, company owners, and other businesspeople have a key role to play. And frankly, they have the most to gain.

Suppose, for example, that companies took it upon themselves to help employees learn how the business makes money. Suppose they asked those employees to quit thinking of themselves as hired hands and start thinking of themselves as trusted partners in the enterprise. Suppose further that companies actually treated employees like trusted partners. Owners and managers would share the kind of information that helps people make good decisions about their work and come up with new ideas. They'd expect employees to begin thinking and acting like partners, looking for ways to save money or better serve customers. And they would pay people like partners, ensuring that employees got a share of the wealth that they were helping create.

There are many ways in which business is a force for good in our society. It delivers products and services that people value. It provides jobs and income, thereby putting food on tables and roofs over heads. But how much more good could it do if it helped everyone on the payroll begin to think and act like partners—like capitalists?

This, it should be noted, is perhaps the perfect example of a win-win situation, as my friend Warren understood. Companies would be more profitable. Individual employees would make more money. Customers would be better served. Managers and workers wouldn't be so mistrustful or hostile, as they were at BHP and have been at so many other companies, because they would be pulling together. Everyone would understand the business they were engaged in, and they would collaborate to make it successful. The people at the top would learn a lot as well, because frontline employees are frequently closest to customers and often have valuable perspectives on how the company can improve.

I like to think that companies would uncover many closet capitalists like Warren—people who come to understand that a company where people are partners is a lot more productive and a lot more remunerative than a company where everyone is just drawing a paycheck. It takes some time to make this happen, but not as much time as you would think. In the case of BHP, six months was a long enough period to create sustainable behavioral change and improved results.

Now, all this may sound like wishful thinking. But the chapters that follow will explain a hard-nosed systematic way—a time-tested methodology—of creating just such a company. Over twenty-five years, I have helped businesses of all sorts implement this system. The list includes publicly traded giants like BHP and Capital One. It also includes a host of midsize companies and entrepreneurial enterprises, most of them privately held. These businesses belong to a broad range of industries, from old-line manufacturing businesses to tech start-ups and health-care inno-vators. At last count, my total number of clients had topped four hundred.

I'm proud of these companies' business track records. An initiative at Southwest Airlines—appropriately called "Plane Smart Business"—generated $2 million in fuel and productivity savings in just six months. A project at Boardman Inc., an Oklahoma manufacturer of pressure vessels, led to a sales increase of 55 percent, with profits totaling more than the company's three previous years combined. At CWT, the trav-el-management company, a pilot project in three branches turned in re-sults $1.7 million above budgeted profit; meanwhile, all the rest of the company's branches were coming in at budget or below. At FA Engineer-ing in Idaho, the staff doubled, the revenue tripled, and profits were up more than 400 percent in two years. I'll mention some other results—in-cluding the occasional disappointment—in later chapters.

But I'm prouder still of what these companies have been able to do for their employees and their communities. Employees at these or-ganizations learned to think differently, to view themselves as partners in the business. They benefited economically. Many of my clients had profit-sharing or stock-ownership programs to start with, but the boost in performance added to the value that employees received. Nearly all the companies created self-funded incentive plans—that's part of the sys-tem—and these plans put anywhere from one or two to thirteen weeks of extra pay per year in the wallets of their workers. That money not only provided employees with more income and greater security; it also helped boost the prosperity of the communities these people lived in. Many of these employees are members of groups that historically hav-en't had great educational or job opportunities. Now they are enjoying the benefits of being full members of a successful business. All that is just a small indication of the power of partnership capitalism.

How can you create such results in your company? We'll get to that shortly. Right now, let's go back to Warren.

## COMMON GROUND

After the meeting, I asked for a follow-up chat. Warren and I exchanged cards, and I noticed that his wasn't the standard BHP variety. "That's my union card," he explained. "I'm president of the union." Later, he invited me to a Labor Party meeting. Despite a few misgivings—I'm not usually a fan of labor-oriented political parties, my great-grandfather notwithstanding—I agreed to go along.

It was a forty-five-minute ride, and we entered the meeting hall just as things were getting underway. The first topic was how to improve the local hospital, which was in desperate need of some diagnostic equipment. Someone proposed a fundraiser, and the members agreed. Next up was the local school, which had no air-conditioning. Warren knew of some burned-out mining fans that could be reconditioned at little expense; he'd check with BHP. The meeting got me thinking about the famous observation from Tip O'Neill, the legendary Speaker of the House of Representatives: "All politics is local."

With twenty minutes left, Warren asked me to speak. My presentation was short. I admitted that I came to the meeting not much of a believer in their ideology. But I respected what they were trying to do: taking responsibility for their local community, trying to leave it better than they found it, addressing whatever challenges arose. I explained that this was precisely what I tried to do with companies: improve business results and the lives of the employees who drive those results. I try to create an environment in which everyone understands the economics of the business and takes personal responsibility for seeing things improve in the best way they can. Partnership, so to speak.

The work with BHP's Iron Division, in Port Hedland, Australia, last-ed eighteen months and created some remarkable results. Starting with the company's seaport operations—the key bottleneck at the time—teams of workers shipped enough "safe tonnes" of ore to get the com-pany back on track with its commitments to customers. (We labeled the objective "safe tonnes" to prevent people from cutting dangerous cor-ners and to reinforce the fact that improved safety would help increase production and reduce costs.) Since so many of BHP's costs were fixed, increasing shipments reduced the company's cost per ton, thus generat-ing $3 million in additional profits.

With the port bottleneck improved, attention moved to the new bot-tleneck, the rail line that brought the ore from BHP's mining operations to the port, a distance of hundreds of kilometers. The program became known as "Luvin' Rail." This led to further improvements in produc-tion, profits, and employee bonuses—and ultimately to a better rapport among employees and managers.

Warren became one of the strongest leaders of the successful eco-nomic engagement efforts at BHP. He became a good friend, and we both learned a lot from our collaboration. He is still a socialist. I am still a capitalist. Our experience may have been a lesson for both of us: the differences that divide us are not as powerful as the common goals that unite us. That's a lesson that Americans are discussing a lot right now, and it's pretty much what this book is about. In each chapter, I'll include a Partnership Principle that encapsulates that chapter's message. (You can find the complete list of these principles in the appendix.) Taken together, the partnership principles provide a recipe for a better business and a better world.

# 1

# THIS IS BUSINESS, SO PARTNERSHIP IS ALL ABOUT THE ECONOMICS

**PLENTY OF COMPANIES** these days seem to want their employees to think and act like trusted partners. You can see the impulse toward workplace partnership in the language now being used in many businesses. Companies call their people associates, team members—anything but employees. Some even use the word partners. You can also see the impulse in the competition for inclusion on various "great places to work" lists featured in the business press and local newspapers. And you can see it in the management philosophies of recent decades—lean, agile, objectives and key results (OKR), self-governing teams, and the like. These methodologies expect employees to take the initiative, to assume new responsibilities, to think for themselves.

You can even see it in the compensation systems many companies have adopted. Performance bonuses, profit sharing, stock options, and so on are tools that executives hope will align everybody's interests so that employees will view themselves as partners rather than just hired hands.

Maybe the most common effort toward creating workplace partnership is the continuing, relentless, almost desperate search for what human resources people call employee engagement. A quick online search on the topic reveals countless books, articles, and tips designed to increase engagement, not to mention the many consulting firms that are peddling sure-fire solutions. According to one estimate, US companies spend $720 million a year on employee engagement programs, internal and external, a number that is projected to rise to $1.5 billion over time. Companies hope that engaged employees will think like owners—like partners—without being told what to do every minute. Most business leaders would love that, at least in theory. The consulting firm Bain & Company recently surveyed about 1,300 executives around the world. More respondents agreed with this statement about management than with any other: "Today's business leaders must trust and empower people, not command and control them." A scant 5 percent disagreed.[12]

Even Walmart, the largest private employer in the US—a company that has long been plagued by troubled relations with its frontline workers—seems to be moving in this direction. In 2020, the retail giant rolled out a framework called "Great Workplace." Dacona Smith, Walmart's chief operating officer, explained it this way: "Across the store, we're creating small teams of associates who will be cross-trained and given ownership of the work and their area. This means they'll gain more skills and be able to support associates who want to take time off or just need extra help during a busy shift."[13]

What's the significance of all this? Are these just nice words, with no tangible meaning behind them? How likely is it that piecemeal changes in language, in managerial techniques, in compensation, and so on will create workplaces where people view themselves as trusted partners in the enterprise and act accordingly?

The record is mixed. I doubt that any employee feels more engaged simply by virtue of being called an associate or a team member. And I have to think that many of the efforts to engage employees are fruitless or downright counterproductive—sort of like the be-nice-and-no-swearing effort at BHP. After all, the statistics on employee engagement have improved only a tiny bit over the course of decades. Nevertheless, some of the moves are undoubtedly steps in the right direction. Every Starbucks or Microsoft or tech start-up that shares equity with its employees helps muddy the stark divisions between owners of capital and people who work for a living. Every company that takes seriously the idea of self-managing teams helps its workers learn to be something more than hired hands. Every company that is majority employee owned—there are several thousand of these in the US now—shows that a different kind of capitalism is possible and that it works in the marketplace.

But there's a larger opportunity here, an opportunity to put flesh on all these well-meaning bones. It's an opportunity to create companies that build partnership into their daily operations, that put all the pieces together and come out with something new. It's an opportunity not just to create great companies but to lay the foundation of a new kind of capitalism, one that includes rather than excludes the great majority of people.

Seizing this opportunity does not mean simply being nicer to employees, though niceness never hurts. Nor does it depend on paying people more, though a wage increase or a bonus is always pleasant for those who receive it. And it doesn't depend at all on company picnics, team-building workshops, free food in the cafeteria, or any of the other goodies that companies dole out in hopes of increasing engagement. Those don't hurt either, so long as a company can afford them. But they are mostly beside the point.

Rather, the opportunity hinges on helping people *understand* and *par-*

*ticipate in* capitalism. In the workplace, that means understanding a business's economics.

Here's why. A business is a particular kind of social institution. Its purpose is to deliver goods and services that customers value, and in the process to make money. It provides its shareholders with a return on their investment. It provides managers and employees with jobs and income. It is an *economic* institution. It is not a school, a church, or a government agency. (These organizations deal with funds and budgets too, of course, but making money is not usually their primary objective.)

The more money a company makes, the better off everyone in the business is likely to be. Even if the employees aren't shareholders, a profitable, growing company is likely to offer better opportunities—for job security, wage increases, skill development, and advancement through the ranks—than one that is struggling. These are basic economic facts.

There's a psychological dimension to making money as well as an economic one. People feel good when their incomes are rising. They are more secure. They can take better care of their families. They can buy more of what they want, and they can save more for retirement or a rainy day. Most of us like making money for all these reasons. Other things equal, most of us would like to make more of it. We have an *economic* interest in the success of the company we work for, whether or not we're the boss.

The job for management, then, is to help people understand that economic interest—and to make it tangible by involving them in furthering the company's success and sharing the wealth that they help create. The job, in short, is to give them a stake in the system and an opportunity to participate in it. You want real engagement? Engage people in making money.

Here's a short list of how you can do this:

1. **Help people learn the basic economics of the business.** Most company employees don't have MBAs. They don't know or care much about accounting. Companies sometimes try to address these limitations by sponsoring in-house classes in financial literacy. Though classes like these can be useful for managers who aspire to senior executive positions, basic classes for rank-and-file employees rarely accomplish much. Because the lessons don't have any relevance to people's jobs, they are soon forgotten.

   Other companies decide that they are going to be "open book." That is, they are going to share full financial statements with employees every month or maybe every quarter. It's a nice gesture, and it reflects the rising interest in open-book management, a philosophy I have long espoused. But if that's all they do, the effect is no greater than a financial-literacy class that everybody soon forgets. Who wants to spend time poring over thick sets of numbers, particularly if you aren't sure what any of the numbers mean?

   The fact is, there's a far better way of helping people understand the company's economics. That will be the subject of chapter 2.

2. **Provide people with a clear way to track, forecast, and improve the company's performance over time.** As any entrepreneur or executive knows, business is a fascinating activity. Every day can bring a new challenge or opportunity. Over time—weeks, months, quarters, eventually years—you can see how your company is doing. Ideally, you are watching it grow, prosper, do a better and better job of serving its customers and making money. If your business is not on that trajectory, you have the interest-

ing and often rewarding challenge of figuring out what has gone wrong and how to turn things around.

Right now, most employees don't get to take part in this process. They don't know how the company they work for is faring. They typically understand little about how their own job or team fits into the big picture. When business seems to be going well, they decide that something—who knows what?—must be working right. When things turn down, they decide that management is a bunch of idiots who don't know what they're doing. When a company announces a layoff—and layoffs seem to crop up in the news almost every week, even when the economy is thriving—most of the people who are affected say they never saw it coming.

So helping employees learn to think like partners in the business means making it possible for everyone to see and understand the economic performance of the company and their team, week in and week out. It means drawing the connections between what people do every day, how they think, how they work, and the company's business results. And it means creating structured opportunities for people to improve the company's performance. Chapter 3 will show you how to build performance tracking, forecasting, learning, and continuous improvement into your everyday operations.

3. **Share the reasons for putting so much effort into understanding and tracking economic performance.** The management methods we'll discuss in this book ask a company to rethink how it operates. They ask employees to learn new ways of thinking and acting. This doesn't have to be a painful process for anybody—in fact, most of the companies that take the partner-

ship approach find that business is a lot more fun than it used to be. Still, it's a change. And people everywhere are often reluctant to change.

You can see this reluctance when companies adopt one or more of the latest management philosophies—lean, agile, OKR—whatever it may be. Suddenly employees are supposed to be thinking and acting differently. They learn new terms, new procedures, new ways of organizing and carrying out work. But the initiatives often run into a wave of eye-rolling and cynicism on the part of frontline employees. And who can blame them? If people don't understand the reason for the new management methods, if they can't see the effects of these methods on business performance and their own opportunities, why on earth should they care? Just so the owners can get richer than they already are? The initiatives wind up foundering on that time-honored response from people everywhere: *What's in it for me?*

So we need to add the *why* to the *what* and the *how*; we need to add the reason to the methodologies. That's where sharing new, incrementally generated wealth comes in. If you ask people to think and act like partners, you better be prepared to compensate them as partners. Otherwise, they'll feel like they're being taken advantage of. And they'd be right. I'll discuss how to share the wealth in chapters 4 and 5. If you do it right, everyone will win—including the company.

Put these three elements together and what you get isn't just a method of engaging more employees or creating a better workplace. It's a fundamentally different way of running a company—a different management system. This idea of a system is important. It's often said that the real problem with the workplace, the reason so few employees are engaged in their work, lies with individual managers. That's why companies spend so much on trying to hire and train the "right" people. I have a different perspective. When people operate in a system that encourages certain kinds of behavior, many more of them turn out to have been exactly the right people all along. When the system gets everyone working together, you don't need charismatic leaders.

Of course, people are people. You may occasionally find a manager who is condescending, who is hopelessly incompetent, or who just doesn't want to get with the program. You may find an employee who has no interest in doing anything other than the bare minimum. Chapters 6 and 7 discuss how to deal with the challenges, external and internal, that can confront a partnership company. But the management system outlined in this book enables more and more people to collaborate effectively and to get things done. When employees become trusted partners, a company's profits rise. Employees' incomes rise. Those are the economic consequences. But the transformation has other effects as well. People pull together. They grow. "B" managers transform into "A" managers. Work becomes more rewarding. Employees become worth more because they know more and generate better results. Everyone feels like part of a team.

Partnership is economic, yes. But it isn't just economic. It's also the right thing to do. And it points us toward a better future.

## AN ENTREPRENEURIAL COMPANY
## LEARNS THE ECONOMICS

Before we get to the practicalities of implementation, let me tell a quick story about learning the economics. It's from a company that's about as different from BHP as you can get and still be in the world of business. It will give you a preview of what you'll find in the chapters that follow.

Angus Beasley and Eric Adams knew one another from their days in middle school English class in Cambridge, Massachusetts. While still in their twenties they created Adams + Beasley Associates (ABA), a high-end remodeling and construction company serving the Boston area. The firm did pretty well, and the young founders had fun. They wanted to run an organization with the same sort of team and family orientation that they had grown up with. Other than that, however, ABA was more or less an ordinary company, and the financial results were less than spectacular. The CEO peer group that the two young men belonged to viewed them as nice guys but not all that great at running a profitable business.

So what was missing? A deep understanding of the business's economics. When they asked me to take them on as a client, my job was to help everyone in the company learn—and then track—how ABA made money.

The starting point was to find the right economic focus. Following what has become standard procedure for my firm—I'll lay out the whole process in chapter 2—the founders and I first solicited anonymous input from employees. What did people see as the company's biggest challenges? Its most significant opportunities? What would they do differently if they were in charge? Questions like these get people involved from the outset, helping to build trust and buy-in. Interviews with managers and the founders themselves added to the insights we got from the employees. Next, we sat down with management and scrutinized the company's financial trends. Where were the strengths and weaknesses, the opportunities and threats? The founders also spoke with current and past customers. What elements of the company's services did those customers value? What could be improved?

At that point, ABA was like a lot of small businesses: it needed improvement in net profit, the proverbial bottom line. But one discovery surprised us. The company's accounting system tracked costs incurred each week and allocated job margin—gross profit earned on each project—based on the percentage of project completion. If a huge volume of materials arrived one month, the accounting system assumed the related projects were that much nearer completion, thus generating a huge gross margin. Net profit bounced around accordingly and did not reflect the actual amount of work done.

So we decided to simplify the economics. For each of the company's jobs, we mapped the start date, the completion date, total expected revenue, and total projected costs. When a change order came in for any aspect of the project, we modified the revenue and costs accordingly. Continually mapping these figures provided a more accurate and up-to-date projected gross margin for each job.

We then developed a scoreboard and began tracking those figures every week. In Monday-morning meetings, we would review the updated start date, completion date, and total gross margin for each job, as reported by the job's project manager. We found that our straight-line approach to tracking job margin was not only more accurate but easier for everyone to understand. Though the company continued producing its standard financial reports, everyone in the organization came to understand that the very high and very low months on those reports were usually just accounting noise. The forecast job-by-job gross margin from the weekly meetings was much more reflective of the true economics of the company and relatively easy for the various project teams to track.

As 2018 began, the company's results looked strong. This meant something to everyone because we had also devised a profit-sharing plan with a payout tied directly to the job-margin dollars the company was earning. (The profit-sharing plan was also the basis for my coaching compensation, so I had a vested interest in the company's success. I learned later that people in the company came to view me as part of the team, a partner, because of this arrangement.) We added the projected bonus to the scoreboard so that every employee could see exactly where they stood.

That's when the magic began to happen. People started tracking the jobs they worked on. They could see whether they were ahead or behind. They began figuring out ways to get the jobs done more effectively and more profitably. And since the bonus was based on total company gross margin dollars, project managers naturally traded ideas on what worked and what didn't.

In the first quarter of the year, the bonus amounted to a couple of weeks of extra pay for everybody—not huge, but enough to get people's attention. By the end of the year, however, the results were notable. The company made more net profit in 2018 than it had in the last ten years combined. Total bonuses paid to ABA employees came to just over seven weeks of pay per person.

Understand, I'm not taking credit for this record performance. The local economy was strong at the time. The founders had been building a friendly, team-oriented, performance-driven culture for years, and they had made many smart business decisions along the way. In fact, I learned as much from them as they may have learned from me, as is usually the case with my clients. All that said, the partnership approach was helping everyone see more clearly how the business worked and how they could improve it.

As we prepared for the following year's plan, several employees expressed concern about such high bonuses. Could the company really afford them? A review of the numbers demonstrated that the bonuses were very well funded, thanks to the improvement in job margin dollars. It also showed that the company was in a far stronger financial position at the end of 2018, even after paying bonuses, than it had been before. But here's the key point: frontline employees were worrying more about the company's financial health than about their own. They were thinking like partners.

Over time, more and more people began to think in this manner. An example was the construction firm's estate-care and small-jobs division, led by a woman named Diane Sills. At the end of each job, the project manager would introduce Di to the customer. She assured the customer that she and her team would be happy to take care of any small issue or project with their home. (The firm had tried this approach a few years earlier but without the focus and commitment that Di was now bringing to it.) The division helped create ongoing relationships between ABA and large customers, virtually assuring that the company would be considered for the next major remodeling program. Moreover, the margin on the small projects and estate-care work, employees found, was usually higher than the margin on the typical large project. That was another factor that inspired everyone to get behind the effort.

Di, however, was thinking long term—like a partner. One week, when it was her turn to give an update, she explained that a small project for a customer had come in surprisingly under budgeted cost. She felt the right thing to do was to refund the customer $5,000, which would reduce the margin but would be a nice gesture. Everyone agreed. The following week, Di reported that the customer who got the $5,000 check hugged her. "She will be an ABA advocate for life in a target neighborhood for us," said Di. Meanwhile, late in 2018, the founders expanded their ownership, offering equity stakes to Nick Beasley, who was responsible for remodeling operations, and Laura Burnes, who was responsible for planning and design. The move showed everyone how acting like a trusted partner could translate into company ownership beyond the bonus plan.

The following year brought more of the same: profits in 2019 broke the record set in 2018. It also brought more partner-like thinking. People began asking themselves what the chances were of a downturn in the Greater Boston real estate market. The firm began to focus even more than before on the estate-care and small-projects business; because customers didn't have to lay out large amounts of money, this part of the business might be less sensitive to a market downturn. The company also offered a commitment to all employees: there would be no layoffs. To back up that commitment, the founders began publishing a regularly updated report showing how many months of employees' salaries could be paid with cash on hand and committed backlog. This company was well on its way to the next level. When the coronavirus struck in 2020, all the caution and concern looked prescient: the company was well positioned to weather the storm.

Of course, ABA is just one small company, and it has been on the partnership journey only a few years. But it illustrates the fundamental lessons that we'll elaborate on in the chapters to come. Understand the economics. Track and improve the company's performance. Share the wealth. Now, let's go on to the practicalities of how to turn hired hands into business partners.

**PARTNERSHIP PRINCIPLE #1**

Partners know their business. They understand the economics.

# 2

## KEY NUMBERS: THE BEST (AND EASIEST) WAY TO LEARN AND TEACH THE ECONOMICS

**PARTNERSHIP RESTS ON** a foundation of economic engagement. Economically engaged employees take joint responsibility with management for helping the company succeed. But not many will feel engaged if they don't know what the business is all about. People need to understand the goal of the enterprise. They need to see how all the different parts fit together and how that creates value. Then they can help it create more value.

So now: Imagine a company that builds this kind of learning, involvement, and accountability into its day-to-day operations. Imagine that the learning and involvement and accountability all deepen over time so that employees eventually come to think and act like businesspeople.

Creating such a company is easier than you might think. It begins with a simple idea, which I call a *key number.* Key numbers are unique to each business. They measure something critical to the business's operation that tracks closely with the results you're after. If you improve your key number, you improve your company's financial performance.

This number is "key" in another sense as well. It's a key that unlocks the door to economic engagement, partnership, and a healthier, more profitable enterprise.

## THE ORIGIN OF KEY NUMBERS

Early in my career, I was serving as vice president of business development at J. I. Case, the manufacturer of agricultural and construction equipment that is now part of CNH Industrial. One day I was asked to visit a company in Missouri known as Springfield ReManufacturing Corporation, or SRC. SRC was a small but innovative supplier, I was told, and Case was contemplating a joint venture with it.

I had heard that SRC's frontline employees were supposed to know a great deal about their company's economics, but I have to admit I was skeptical. When I came across a factory worker polishing crankshaft journals, I decided to ask him a question.

"Good morning," I said. "My name is Bill Fotsch. If you don't mind, I have a question for you. I'm aware that most SRC employees really understand their business. So I'm curious: What is the price of that crankshaft you are working on?" At Case, I thought, such a question would probably provoke a grievance for trying to embarrass a union worker. I figured I'd get no answer and that I'd probably wind up explaining the difference between price and cost. (If I sound arrogant, chalk it up to my youth.)

The worker looked up. "List price or dealer net?" he asked. Then he went on to explain both prices, how they compared with SRC's cost, and what his own component of the cost was.[†]

---

[†]  I first told this story to my collaborator, John Case, who included it in his book *Open-Book Management*.

That was pretty impressive. So I promptly learned more about SRC. The company was previously a division of International Harvester (now Navistar International) and had recently been bought by a team led by the plant manager, Jack Stack. But its debt load was heavy and its existence precarious. If it ran out of cash to make the loan payments, it would go under. So Stack's team had taken it upon themselves to educate every worker and every manager in the plant about the importance of cash. They tracked cash levels daily and publicly. They devised ways of cutting cash expenditures and of collecting receivables faster. Everyone knew their jobs were at stake and that the key to survival was cash.

Over the years, SRC expanded and deepened this system, focusing first on one key financial number and then, when that one was well in hand, on another. At each stage, everyone in the company learned what the number meant and how they themselves could move the needle in the right direction.[‡] That's why the worker I spoke to was so knowledgeable. SRC attracted a good deal of attention from other businesspeople and began to help others learn this approach. I formed a joint venture with Stack, and for nineteen years I worked with companies to help them apply these principles. In 2012 I launched my own firm to pursue the same kind of work, but with a bit more focus on customers, since customers define value and therefore a company's economics.

## A KEY NUMBER ILLUMINATES A CLEAR GOAL

SRC was in desperate straits when it started out because of its mammoth debt load. So it was easy for Stack's team to identify cash as the company's key number. But nearly every company or division within any

---

[‡] You can learn more about SRC and its methods in the classic book *The Great Game of Business*, by Jack Stack and Bo Burlingham.

company can identify one number that is critical to the business and that managers and employees can learn to understand and track. In a company with relatively simple economics, such as a restaurant, the number can be correspondingly simple—gross margin percentage, say, or gross profit dollars. One fast-food franchisee I learned about began posting simplified income statements on the wall every week so that his teenage workers could track how much gross profit the franchise was making. Project-based companies such as Adams + Beasley can track job-margin dollars, or gross profit contributed by each job. Professional services firms often find it useful to track billable hours per person, a figure that typically links directly to their profitability. In all these cases, improvement in the key number automatically produces better economic results. That's an essential element of any key number.

In larger companies, it may seem more difficult to find key numbers that link directly to financial results. But if you focus on the local economics of a given team or unit, the process turns out to be pretty much the same as in smaller companies, with results that are just powerful.

Southwest Airlines, for example, was coping at one point with a steep rise in the price of jet fuel, which was hurting its profitability. So operational managers joined with the pilots' union to propose a joint initiative based on key-number principles. The initiative—dubbed Plane Smart Business—began with a group of six hundred pilots based at the company's station in Orlando, Florida. These pilots began tracking their fuel usage closely. They drew on the tricks of their trade to reduce it, including flying a perfect profile (getting to elevation more quickly); coordinating with ground crews to get to gates rapidly and connect to local power; and being more conscientious about avoiding storms to reduce unnecessary fuel burn. One innovative idea was to add life rafts to Houston–Miami flights, allowing the airline to fly a direct route over the Gulf of Mexico. This not only saved fuel but shortened the flight by thirty minutes, which made it popular with passengers. The six-month effort led to $2 million in fuel and productivity savings, an amount that increased with subsequent implementation.

Here's another example. A few years ago, Carlson Wagonlit, the global travel-management company now known as CWT, decided to conduct a controlled experiment. At the time, the company operated twenty-seven branches in North America, each one responsible for clients in its region and accountable to the parent company for certain profit targets. The parent decided to launch an initiative based on the key-number principle at three of its branches while leaving the others operating as before. Following a process that I'll describe in a moment, the experimental branches developed a consensus regarding the critical issues they faced during the next six to twelve months. They also developed a metric—direct profitability, or revenue minus direct costs—that would indicate their performance. Employees began brainstorming about how to improve results, sharing information and forecasts at weekly meetings. After a year, the outcome could scarcely have been clearer. The three experimental branches exceeded their annual profit targets by 10 percent, 17 percent, and 20 percent after incentive payments. None of the other twenty-four branches achieved its profit target that year. Not surprisingly, the company rolled out the engagement process to the rest of the branches, based on the success of the three experimental branches.

Like CWT, any large company with branches, stores, or separate business units may decide to use some measure of profitability as a key number. But even units traditionally thought of as cost centers are candidates for effective key-number management. I learned this several years ago when I was working with Capital One, the big US bank.

Capital One at the time maintained its own back-office operations, known as Production Services. This unit performed a wide variety of tasks—imaging, payment processing, correspondence, and so on. A classic cost center, it was traditionally managed to meet a budget handed down from on high.

But the manager in charge of the unit, Dan Mortensen, was developing a different vision. What if Production Services thought of itself as its own company? Its customers were the bank's other divisions. Its competitors were the specialized outsourcers that the bank might otherwise have to rely on. With the approval of senior executives, Mortensen launched an initiative he called Committed, Engaged Owners, or CEOs. For each of the various cost centers reporting to him, he and his team developed a single number to track, such as cost per account (CPA), and a goal for lowering it. Those simple numbers gave everyone in the division a means to benchmark their operations. Financial staff began figuring out how to track costs more efficiently and more quickly. Managers scrutinized their budgets to ensure that the costs they were responsible for stayed in line. Frontline employees and supervisors took the initiative as well; an "efficiency improvement team," for instance, promptly came up with more than a dozen significant process improvements, projecting close to $750,000 in annual cost savings.

This way of thinking began spilling out into some of the bank's other cost centers. The training unit, for instance—traditionally evaluated by the number of people trained and by budgeted costs—now began evaluating itself by how much it could contribute to Production Services' cost goals. "I'm actually getting CPA data from all of our clients on a weekly basis," the training director told me, "and I'm using that data in our weekly manager meetings." One of her staff created a series of modules for Production Services' document management unit focusing on critical drivers of CPA, such as turnaround time.

In a large company, it helps to keep a couple of guidelines in mind when you're developing a key number. You want to deconstruct the company into all of the smaller businesses that make it up. A "business" in this case is any department, branch, or unit that has a common objective. It should have fewer than five hundred employees—ideally, fewer than 250—so that it can operate as a single team. And you should concentrate initially on areas in which improvement will have the most benefit: a manufacturing bottleneck, for example, or a critical source of customer complaints.

## WHY A KEY NUMBER WORKS

One big advantage of a key number is that it defines *winning*.

Most people in a company don't know whether the business is winning or losing at any given time. They just do their jobs. Business performance is somebody else's responsibility. Even managers—who are supposed to track their unit's or company's results—may get swamped by the deluge of financial and operational statistics that many companies provide. I once worked with a unit of a large telecommunications company, one of the group that used to be known as Baby Bells. The manager I was meeting with pulled out a sheaf of reports with dozens of different statistics and metrics, some of which traded off with each other (customer satisfaction versus time per service call, for example). When I asked her for the bottom line—was the unit's performance getting better or worse over time?—she sighed. "I wish you'd tell me," she said.

Statistics don't lie, so it is said, but they don't inspire most people either. A key number, by contrast—a simple metric that everyone understands and tracks from week to week—shows you whether you are winning or losing right now. And winning has a way of engaging people.

You want to see that line heading upward on the graph! When something happens that boosts results, people feel great. Meetings break out into spontaneous applause. When the opposite happens, it's like falling behind in a game of basketball—you try harder. You figure out what you need to do differently. Either way, the ability to know whether you're winning or not builds camaraderie and team spirit.

It's amazing to me how many companies miss out on this simple idea. Sure, they may use metrics like key performance indicators, or KPIs. But KPIs typically create a mishmash of incentives and goals. They divide people rather than unite them. When I was with BHP in Australia, the division I worked with actually had 203 separate KPIs, each one linked to its own bonus plan. Hit your KPI and you get extra money. But the KPIs pitted employees and departments against one another. The parts department's KPI was minimizing the money tied up in spare-parts inventory. The production department's KPI was throughput. Not surprisingly, when a machine went down, the parts required for repair were frequently unavailable. That not only stalled production; it also soured relationships between the departments. When the division began pursuing a single common objective—safe tonnes shipped—the different units had an incentive to work together. Now everyone could tell when the whole team was winning. So here's the next Partnership Principle:

### PARTNERSHIP PRINCIPLE #2

Partners have a clear line of sight. They know whether the business is winning or losing.

There's another big advantage of key numbers too. As people track a key number over time, they begin to understand the company's economics.

Think about it. If you're a frontline employee tracking gross profit or job margin or service costs, you have a window into the way the business works. You learn that it really matters to operate efficiently, to save money where you can, to come up with ideas for offering better service. And not just that—you see *how much* it matters because you watch the number change. When the needle moves in one direction or the other, you begin to ask questions. Why are we getting better? What happened to cause that slippage? Managers, sales reps, engineers, senior leaders—they all learn that they better explain what's going on so that people throughout the organization can take appropriate actions. For the employees, watching the number is like an ongoing course in business, one that actually affects what they do every day on the job.

## DEVELOPING THE KEY NUMBER

Some of my clients ask me to tell them what their key number should be, even before I have spent time with them. Very often, companies assume that the key number is net profit. They seem to think that a key number should be like an adjustable baseball cap—one size fits all. But nothing could be further from the truth.

For one thing, every industry is different. Companies with a high proportion of fixed costs—professional service firms, hotels, airlines—make the most money when their people and assets are fully utilized. Manufacturers make the most money when they increase production efficiency without compromising quality or customer service. Companies in fast-changing industries like technology do best when they introduce popular innovations. So key numbers will naturally vary from one industry to another.

Business strategies differ as well. Tiffany & Co. faces a different set of constraints and opportunities than Dollar Store. An insurance broker-age focusing on corporate clients with complex needs will run its busi-ness differently from one whose customers are mainly homeowners and drivers. Key numbers necessarily reflect a company's strategic priorities.

One useful approach to key-number development—one that nat-urally incorporates your industry's constraints and your own strategic priorities—is to consider what your company's most pressing challenges and opportunities are right now. Say that you run a restaurant, or may-be a chain of restaurants. There are plenty of numbers restaurateurs typically track, including gross margin, the ratio of food or labor costs to total costs, number of customers served, average tab per table, and so on. Ask yourself: In your business, are any of these numbers out of whack right now, really in need of improvement? If so, that one might be a good candidate for key number.

But here's the real secret to developing a key number: don't rely on your intuition alone. This is about engagement and partnership, after all. You want to get everyone in your business involved, right from the beginning. And believe me: the process of creating a key number is every bit as important as the number itself.

When my colleagues and I take on a client, we begin by gathering four kinds of information: input from employees, input from managers, financial data, and the views of customers.

The surveys of employees and managers ask respondents what they see as the company's biggest challenges and opportunities for the next six to twelve months. We ask them to pinpoint what they think could be improved. These are important questions, and the people responding to the surveys begin to feel like trusted partners in the business. The surveys also turn up useful information. At Gasper Corporation, an Ohio-based application software company that would later be sold to NCR, sales per employee seemed like a logical key number. But several people in the development department pointed out that most of the current year's sales came from features developed the previous year. If the company focused only on current sales per employee, it might underinvest in new feature development, which would hurt future sales. So Gasper ended up going with two metrics. One was an adapted version of revenue per employee, which excluded employees who worked in development. The development department, meanwhile, created a metric that accounted for the market value per developer of every new feature that was incorporated in the software.

In the surveys, it is always interesting to compare the managers' insights with those of the employees. Often they're pretty much in sync. But sometimes the two groups focus on very different things—usually a sign that communication in the company isn't as good as it should be. For example, management might be concentrating on opening up a new market, while employees are seeing problems with serving existing customers.

With the surveys complete, we get together with senior management and review the company's financials for the past five years. Let me tell you: sometimes the financials are screaming! Maybe gross margin has been steadily dropping. Maybe general and administrative (G&A) costs have been rising faster than sales. Maybe the cost of fixing production errors—rework—is way above industry standards. Problems like these can creep into any company over time, often without management really being aware of it. But the financials definitely don't lie, and they can sometimes show you exactly where the most pressing challenges and the biggest opportunities are to be found. If the financials reveal a heavy debt load and negative cash flow, for instance, you better focus on cash or you won't survive.

Finally, we get customer input, typically through a series of phone calls with representative customers. We suggest that the callers probe a little to really understand the customers' views. What do the customers value most about doing business with the company? What really annoys them? What new products or services would they like to see the company develop? What are competitors offering that this company doesn't? The process often turns up important discoveries. FA Engineering, for instance—a company you'll meet in the following chapter—learned that its customers really valued the firm's scanning technology, which could provide a 3D layout of an entire plant.

The process of setting your key number may seem unnecessarily detailed, but it's essential. And it has three big payoffs:

1. **The process involves frontline employees as partners right from the beginning.** We often find that our survey is the first time the company has ever asked their opinions about anything. Now they are getting a chance to offer input. It's the first step toward creating a feeling of partnership. And it increases the chance that employees at every level will eventually understand and buy into the key number that the company develops.

2. **It examines the business analytically and begins identifying what needs to be changed.** A lot of companies, we find— even big ones—mostly go on doing today what they did yesterday and the day before that. And that's fine, as long as (a) the market is stable and (b) competitors aren't threatening and (c) unnoticed problems aren't weakening the business. But how often do all three conditions hold?

3. **Finally, those talks with customers? They tend to impress the people who do business with you.** They put your

company top of mind. They nearly always generate a good deal of repeat and referral business. Most companies decide to continue these conversations on a regular basis even after establishing their key number.

When you're considering a particular key number, make sure it addresses the various issues you face. If you can, ensure that it has both a cost component and a revenue component, such as revenue per paid hour. Finally, keep it as simple as possible. There are no points for needless complexity.

So yes: it's worth putting in all this time and effort. The key number, after all, lays the groundwork for the rest of the system I'll outline in this book. It's a metric you'll be living for a while, so it better be right.

## CHANGING THE KEY NUMBER

Of course, "a while" isn't forever. Business conditions change. Companies change. If you are successful in improving a key number, you may find that you don't need to focus on it so closely. You may also find that there's another element of the business that merits attention. Remember Jack Stack and his employees at SRC? In the early days they focused on cash, out of necessity. But their company was successful, and soon it was generating enough cash to make the payments on that initial debt. Eventually, the debt was retired. Cash, by itself, was no longer a problem. At that point SRC could and did focus on other metrics, such as profitability.

A company's annual planning process is a good time to reexamine a key number. Repeat the same foundational steps—gathering input from employees, managers, financials, and customers—and ask yourself several questions. Has the key number been a good one, easily understandable by all and directly linked to business results? Have people learned how to move it in the right direction? Is it time now to focus on another weakness or opportunity? A distribution company that has been concentrating on profitability might want to dig deeper into its operations and focus on, say, inventory turns. That restaurant might move from an emphasis on cost control to an emphasis on getting more people in the door or increasing the size of the average tab.

Changing the number in this way deepens everyone's understanding of the business. People learn the components of profit. They begin to see more connections between day-to-day operations and financial results. Understanding the business becomes a kind of ongoing adventure, with the learning built in. It's a week-in, week-out course in business economics that everyone participates in.

## JUST ONE NUMBER? REALLY?

By now you may be asking yourself a skeptical question: Is this guy really saying you can run a business by looking at only one metric? That you should forget about all the other indicators that company owners and managers typically track?

Of course not. The folks in finance should continue to calculate return on assets, return on equity, days sales outstanding, inventory turns, and all the other ratios that make a financial analyst's heart beat faster. Manufacturing managers will monitor quality, safety, on-time delivery, and so on. Marketers can watch customer satisfaction, customer churn, and the like. Executives at larger companies may continue to use balanced scorecards, executive dashboards, and other tools of modern management. The point of a key number isn't to eliminate every other metric. The point is to show everyone in the company whether they are winning or losing at business—this week, this month, this quarter, and this year. The point is to engage them in understanding the fundamentals of the business so that they can make good decisions and feel part of a common economic enterprise. The key number establishes priorities and thus indicates the relative importance of other metrics.

Key numbers, like any other metric, require management. Suppose a company is tracking operating profit or gross margin per job. Employees may be tempted to cut corners, to focus on the short term at the expense of the long. Part of management's job is to remind people about the importance of long-term thinking. It doesn't do any good to increase profit in the short term if you are compromising safety or quality, taking unfair advantage of customers, or exploiting your community (say, by polluting a river). This is the internet age. Word gets out. Companies that take short cuts like these find it hard to keep their customers or attract talented employees. They may find themselves scrutinized by regulators and local officials. In the long run, it never pays to have a bad reputation. Encouraging employees to update forecasts several months out reinforces a long-term perspective.

Employees are likely to understand the importance of long-term thinking; after all, that's how most people live their lives. They invest in homes. They invest in education. And they depend mightily on their jobs. They want the company they work for to be around and to be successful in five and ten and thirty years, not just today.

## A DISAPPOINTMENT!

I said at the beginning of this book that I would share some disappointments as well as some accomplishments with you, all in the interest of complete transparency. No system is perfect, and no effort to change a company always works out exactly as you hoped. So here's one that didn't work out: that Baby Bell I mentioned earlier in this chapter. My experience there does illustrate the advantages of a key number. But it also illustrates one of the things that can go wrong, particularly in a large organization.

The project began with a meeting between myself and an executive named Bob Knowling, whom I came to respect a great deal. I met Bob at the University of Chicago Business School, where we were both guest lecturers. He was the company's chief operating officer at the time, and he was intrigued by the whole partnership approach. So he hired my colleagues and me to develop an initiative.

We began with the unit known as service order provisioning, or SOP. This part of the company was responsible for filling new orders, making sure the customers got dial tones on their phones (remember those?) and all the specific features they had requested. Bob suggested we start at the unit's Cleveland office. That's where I met the manager whom I mentioned earlier, and where I learned that all the metrics she was supposed to track were just confusing her. As for the employees, well, they had no idea what goals they might be shooting for. They just did as they were told.

So we went through the process I have outlined, and we agreed on a simple, easily understandable metric: cost per order provisioned. The division had never focused on this one number before. We got Bob to agree that if an SOP center improved its cost per order, no one would be laid off. That had been one of the employees' main concerns. Fortunately, demand for the company's services was rising, so it wasn't difficult for the company to guarantee job security.

Over six months, we had a lot of successes. Costs dropped. The employees got involved. Eventually all thirteen of the unit's branches adopted the key-number approach. They traded notes with one another, accelerating the learning and improvement. Six months in, for instance, the Milwaukee office pointed out that the company's marketing department would often come up with a new service but not take the time to automate the provisioning. That resulted in a lot of manual effort and consequently higher cost per order. To address this, Milwaukee developed a novel solution. Instead of insisting that marketing spend the time and money to create automated provisioning, they gave marketing a choice: higher costs to support manual provisioning or lower costs if marketing automated the provisioning. Learning from Milwaukee, other units took a similar approach. In effect, they were treating marketing like a customer, thus benefiting the entire company.

One day, however, Bob Knowling told me that he had taken a position as CEO at one of this company's competitors. It was a big step up for him, so no one begrudged him the move. And he had arranged to pay us for our work six months in advance, on the pretext that he had a budget surplus that year and didn't know what the following year would bring. So we continued our work for another six months, again with many successes.

Finally I was invited to make a presentation to the company's board, and I asked a couple of employees to accompany me. We outlined the accomplishments and described everything we proposed to do going forward. The board listened, but unenthusiastically—I wasn't sure why. They promised to get back to me.

And then, not long after, I got a call from one of the field techs I had been working with. "Bill," he said, "they are shutting this down. They're no longer providing the information we need to track our performance." I asked why in the world they would be doing that. The only thing this tech knew was that the new CEO wanted no part of "this Knowling program." Evidently Bob had anticipated such a reaction, which is why he decided to pay us six months in advance.

So all our work came to an abrupt end. Later, the CEO who had discontinued the project was forced out of the company as the result of a merger. He got a $40 million severance package. A lot of my friends, the people I worked with, were laid off. That's the way capitalism sometimes works. As the Bible puts it, "For whoever has, to him more shall be given; and whoever does not have, even what he has shall be taken away from him."[14]

But things don't need to work like this. Let's continue with our examination of how to transform a business so that it rewards everybody, not just a few at the top.

# 3

# BUILDING PARTNERSHIP: TRACKING, FORECASTING, AND IMPROVING THE KEY NUMBERS

**EMPOWERMENT HAS LONG** been a buzzword in business. Companies want their employees to take more responsibility, make more decisions on their own, and operate without close supervision. They try to "empower" the employees to do all this.

It's a noble ideal, no doubt. But if employees don't understand the economics of the business, what's the likelihood that they will make good decisions? For that matter, how confident would they be to make *any* decision on their own? Empowered workers might come up with killer innovations or cool ideas for saving money. But if they had no idea whether their proposals made good business sense, they would probably keep their mouths shut. Businesses are organizations based on improving their economics. Empowerment without economic understanding isn't worth much.

That's why a key number is so valuable. It puts people on a path toward understanding the business. It gives them a method for tracking the effects of their decisions and their ideas. Over time, it gets employees not just engaged but *economically* engaged. It helps turn them into business partners.

To see how a company uses a key number to build true empowerment, take a look at FA Engineering, an entrepreneurial professional services firm in Pocatello, Idaho—the "Gateway to the West," as the city is known.

## EMPOWERING ENGINEERS

Richard Feuerborn started the company back in 2011, christening it Feuerborn Associates Engineering (FAE). By the end of that year he had a staff of nine, including a new partner named Jeff Andrews. Both Feuerborn and Andrews were experienced industrial engineers, and they wanted to build a company where everyone felt like trusted partners. I began working with them in 2012.

FAE grew rapidly in those early years. Two manufacturers in particular were offering more and more work to the fledgling firm, to the point where they came to represent nearly 80 percent of FAE's business. In retrospect it was worrisome to be so dependent on just two customers. But everybody at FAE was too busy getting the work done to spend much time fretting. Besides, both customers assured FAE that they would have engineering work available for years.

Then came the plunge. Ironically, it was early in 2013, just as the US economy was again expanding after the financial crisis. But for reasons of their own, FAE's two major customers began cutting back. It turned out that they didn't need as much in the way of engineering services as they had before, and certainly far less than they or FAE had expected. The firm's revenue forecast for January of that year dropped below

$50,000, not enough to keep the company alive.

What happened next? I won't keep you in suspense. FAE soon rebounded. By 2019 it had a staff of over forty, revenue of $4.5 million, and an increase in revenue per hour and consequently net profit. But the interesting part of the story isn't just the bare facts; it's *how* FAE survived the plunge and got back on the track to growth—and how it runs its business today. It's a company that knows exactly where it is headed and how it will get there.

Soon after its inception, FAE began operating with a key number. Feuerborn's team and I did the initial surveys and other diagnostic work described in the previous chapter. We tentatively agreed on revenue per paid hour as the key metric. Since most of the firm's costs were fixed in the short term, revenue per paid hour would almost certainly link directly to profitability. We confirmed the connection by examining profit relative to revenue per hour by month over the previous twelve months, and indeed we found a strong correlation. More to the point, everyone knew how improving revenue per paid hour drove the economics of the business. In sports terms, it contained both an offensive and a defensive component. Revenue was offense—bringing business in the door. The paid hours component was defense, ensuring that costs remained under control. At first the company's revenue per paid hour was about forty dollars.

FAE began tracking its key number every week in an all-hands meeting. People who were on the road called in. The only acceptable excuse for missing the meeting was a conference with a client. Participants went down the list of current customers, reporting on the status of each client's work and forecasting revenue for the coming month. Katie, the office manager, updated the hours forecast so that everyone could see the updated forecast of the key number for the firm as a whole. From there, people could see the bonus forecast associated with the updated key-number forecast. Before long, the meeting was producing a three-month rolling forecast.

When the 2013 plunge came, FAE didn't lay anyone off, so revenue per hour naturally plummeted. Everyone could see that the firm had a lot of underutilized time and that the key to recovery was putting that time to productive use. I had developed a script for my clients to use when reaching out to customers, and I suggested that everyone on the staff who wasn't otherwise occupied begin calling current and former customers, using the script. Of course, mechanical engineers aren't necessarily the most extroverted people in the world, so we encountered a good deal of resistance to the idea. But the numbers were up there for everyone to see, and they were hard to argue with. If you wanted to keep your job, you better begin calling.

After a few role-played internal calls, the staff started making calls to customers and prospects. The following week's meeting was astonishing. Among them, group members had conducted nine customer interviews over the course of a week. The conversations yielded two proposal opportunities and eight referrals to other companies that might be able to use FAE's services. The good work the company had done in the past was paying off. One thing customers particularly valued, as I mentioned earlier, was FAE's scanning technology. Frequently, the customers' own drawings of their plants and facilities were out-of-date. But FAE, using state-of-the-art laser measurements and software analysis, could provide a 3D picture of a plant exactly as it was today, and do it faster than the competition. As the customer calls continued, the engineers learned to market this part of FAE's capabilities.

As 2013 went on, the weekly meetings began to reveal a healthy sign: the revenue graph that had turned so sharply downward in the beginning of the year was beginning to edge back up. By the end of the year, the company had recovered from its weak first quarter and in fact had increased revenue by more than 30 percent—and now no single customer was making up more than 20 percent of total revenue. Most important, revenue per hour had risen from forty dollars to fifty-two dollars. This kind of profitable growth would continue right through 2019, with revenue per hour eventually hitting sixty-four dollars.

If you could sit in on one of FAE's weekly meetings, it might seem at first like any other company staff meeting. There's the coffee. There's the initial joking and small talk. But then, when the numbers go up on the board, you'd see what the meeting is all about. The board shows revenue by customer—budget, forecast, and actual. It shows hours worked. And of course it shows the key number: revenue per paid hour. Every customer entry on the scoreboard has an engineer's name attached to it, and that individual is responsible for alerting the staff about what's coming down the pike. Is work on schedule and on budget? Is there another project that's likely to land next month? How likely? Out of such hands-on detail comes the firm's extraordinarily accurate forecast—a forecast that everyone in the company sees and understands. And everyone likes to see the updated bonus forecast at the end of the meeting.

By the way, another key metric tracked at the meeting is the dollar value of outstanding proposals. If that number drops below a certain level—call it X—the firm knows that it's time to put the sales-and-marketing efforts into high gear. The engineers themselves are still the sales staff; they now call past and present customers regularly. By reaching out to customers on an ongoing basis, they have learned the skills of a sales rep, such as highlighting the firm's ability to take on knotty problems, scrolling through their contact lists when necessary to identify prospects, and asking existing customers for introductions to people at those customers' other facilities.

If the dollar value of outstanding proposals rises to twice X, conversely, people understand something else: they better begin thinking about expanding the company's capacity, either by hiring or, even better, by finding ways to be more efficient. That's a different kind of problem, but it's equally important.

At the beginning, Richard Feuerborn and Jeff Andrews handled most of the sales efforts and quote development themselves. At this writing, there are twelve engineers bringing in proposals. Engineer Jeremy Phelps was so effective at this that the partners offered him an ownership stake, which showed everyone else the route to getting equity in the company. FAE now has a whole group of entrepreneurs—trusted partners—who know what's involved in running the business and who pitch in to do their part. Everyone, from engineer to owner, is actively participating in the continual improvement of their company. That's what I think of as real empowerment. It's encapsulated in the third principle:

### PARTNERSHIP PRINCIPLE #3

Partners take responsibility for improvement. They value different points of view, and they hold each other accountable for results.

## FROM ENGAGEMENT TO PARTNERSHIP

FAE's story illustrates three central elements that lead from the key number to engagement, empowerment, and eventual partnership.

1.  **The key number itself provides a window into the economics of the business.** As I've noted, getting people involved in determining the number is critical. It contributes to understanding and

buy-in.

2. **Tracking the number from week to week through a scoreboard ensures that everyone can follow it.** The scoreboard can be a big whiteboard in a conference room, a simple spreadsheet on a computer screen, or some combination. It can track not just the key number but other variables that drive the key number and the business's health, like FAE's backlog. It should show the budgeted figures, actuals to date, and the latest forecast. But remember KISS: Keep it simple, stupid. The scoreboard should be instantly comprehensible to every employee.

3. **Forecasting results inspires everyone involved.** Once employees begin tracking the number and discussing the factors that affect its movements, they can begin estimating what it will be next month. And once their month-out forecasts are more or less accurate, they can extend those forecasts to three months or more. A forecast is essential because it indicates what is coming down the road. It gets everyone thinking about cause and effect. It identifies potential issues and opportunities before they are on top of you.

Incidentally, many of the clients I have worked with were initially skeptical about forecasting. *Our business is different,* they would tell me. *We can't know what the next few months will hold.* To which I politely respond: bunk. Try it. Sure, there's a learning curve. But you will be amazed at how quickly people learn to identify the key variables and assess the variables' impact on the key number. Once FAE's engineers were up to speed, actuals tracked forecasts remarkably closely. That's how it has been at most of the companies I have worked with.

The tracking and forecasting happen at a regular weekly meeting. Smaller companies (or small units of large businesses) may invite the entire staff. Larger ones may invite representatives who then report back to their units. Offsite employees can attend virtually. This meeting should be short. Its purpose is to share information relating to the key number, nothing more and nothing less. If it turns up issues that need to be addressed or opportunities that need to be capitalized on, those should be discussed separately. The meeting should generate ongoing learning.

These weekly meetings have a special flavor. People come to see what the key number is doing. They pay close attention. They may burst out in applause or hollers if the results are good. In other words, it isn't your typical boring business meeting. What people learn there *matters*—and everyone knows both *what* matters and how *they* matter. Once a month, moreover, people pay extra-close attention. That is when the actuals for the prior month become available. The actuals are compared to forecast. The variances, up or down, provide learning opportunities. The goal is to reach a point where everyone knows what the key number is going to be well in advance. When that is the case, the company is in control of its destiny.

## TRANSLATING INFORMATION INTO ACTION

Knowledge may be power, but it doesn't mean anything until it informs what people do. People may be engaged in learning how their key number is doing, but they won't be empowered until they figure out how to make it move in the right direction. Rather than telling people how to do this, the key number defines winning in a way that allows folks to figure out solutions for themselves. I've seen—and helped implement—a variety of methods for translating knowledge into action.

One method is simplicity itself: brainstorming. Once employees know what the key number is and how they can affect it, they can get together to come up with ideas. Southwest's pilots brainstormed ways to save fuel and then began implementing some of them on their own, without any involvement on the part of higher-ups. The travel agents at those Carlson Wagonlit branches brainstormed ways to generate more revenue and lower their costs, and then began taking the necessary steps. When something worked, they shared their experience with other branches.

Sometimes an outside coach can help. I'm not sure FAE's engineers would ever have decided on their own to call customers. When I suggested it, they were reluctant. But when they got on board, they discovered how useful the idea could be.

Companies may also set up ad hoc improvement teams. In addition to their brainstorming, Southwest's pilot group created teams to investigate specific fuel-saving opportunities, such as tankering—buying fuel at a lower-cost location and carting it to a higher-cost one. Capital One's efficiency improvement team, mentioned earlier, was just one among the many groups Production Services set up to investigate opportunities. Boardman, the Oklahoma-based manufacturer, gathered ideas from all its employees once the key number was identified, then conducted business literacy classes centered on the value of specific ideas.

The most powerful effects often come when companies already have formal continuous-improvement systems in place. For an example of that, let's look at a business that's very different from FAE.

## EMPOWERMENT AT A STEEL FABRICATOR

Trinity Products LLC is a steel pipe manufacturer and custom fabricator headquartered in O'Fallon, Missouri, a half hour's drive west from St. Louis's Lambert International Airport. Trinity makes big, infrastructure-size pipes and structures; you can see the company's handiwork in everything from bridges and power plants to giant signs and scoreboards.

It employs about 180 people and in 2019 did over $100 million in annual revenue.[15] The company's journey began humbly enough. "We started out with fifteen thousand dollars, buying and selling steel," remembers cofounder and current CEO Robert Griggs. That business grew, and in 2006 the company broke ground for a new $10 million spiral pipe mill.

But even from the beginning, Griggs wasn't an ordinary entrepreneur; he had larger goals in mind. "We have three core values in our company," he says, ticking them off on his fingers. "One is that we have a boss, and it's our customer. If we serve our customer every day, we'll all have jobs. Two, we serve our employees by sharing the profit. If we can make our people's lives better, help fulfill their dreams, they'll serve our boss better. And three, continuous improvement. A relentless pursuit of it, every day, every week. It never stops."

Griggs's first step was to help employees learn about the company's revenues, costs, and profits. Trinity circulates a scoreboard every morning showing the key numbers of billings and backlogs by product or process, along with other monthly statistics, such as total orders and total mill tons. Note that these are not the company's financial statements; they are the factors that drive the financials, and they are numbers the employees naturally relate to. But the real question was how employees could use this information to make Trinity's operations more efficient. "We can only control trying to get better," says Griggs. "That lets us feel successful even in years when we don't make much money."

Griggs and his COO, Jim Nazzoli, began working with the Cycle of Success Institute (COSi), a coaching firm that helps small and midsize companies improve. Today, "COSi" has become sort of a watchword at Trinity, reflecting an extraordinary companywide effort to address bottlenecks and obstacles in virtually every element of its operations. The process creates a daily forum where employees can bring forward improvement opportunities, effectively operationalizing the key number.

"You identify a problem, put it on a list, monetize it, and prioritize it," explains Nazzoli, who has added the title of chief continuous improvement officer to his COO job description. High-priority projects are assigned to a team, and every two weeks each team leader reports back to the COSi steering committee on its progress.

"We've accomplished nearly two hundred projects over nine years," adds Griggs. "We have all the data. We took coil splices from twenty-five minutes to fifteen. Changeovers from one size to the next size went from eight hours to five and then to three or three and a half. We continuously organize and prioritize the projects. The ideas never stop and the lists never go away."

Together, the key-number tracking and the COSi project prioritization approach have had a dramatic effect on the attitudes and engagement levels of Trinity's workforce. For example, compare the results of internal employee surveys for 2012 and 2020. Figure 3.1 shows the percentage of employees who responded positively to a sample of questions. And note the questions that showed the biggest improvements with increases of more than twenty percentage points:

*Are managers well qualified to be in their positions?*

*Does the company provide you with continual training in areas that will make you a better employee?*

*Are your responsibilities generally well planned and organized?*

*Does ownership completely understand your work problems?*

*Do you feel updated as to what is happening in the company?*

*Are the customers of the company pleased with the level of quality and service your company provides?*

*Does each department in this company have measurable standards designed to increase profitability?*

*Everything considered, is the company changing for the better?*

Overall, employee responses were significantly more positive in the 2020 survey, averaging 83 percent positive responses for the twenty-six questions compared to 65 percent in 2012. The improvements directly reflect the company's investments in key-number management and continuous improvement.

**Figure 3.1 Trinity Survey**

| | 2012 | | 2020 | | 20% or better |
|---|---|---|---|---|---|
| **People/Culture** | **Yes** | **No** | **Yes** | **No** | 85% or better |
| Are employees in the company comfortable talking to supervisors about work-related probelms? | 76% | 24% | 86% | 14% | 10% |
| Are managers well qualified to be in their positions? | 52% | 48% | 88% | 12% | 36% |
| Are owners/managers open and honest with employees? | 73% | 27% | 88% | 12% | 15% |
| Does the company provide you with continual training in areas that will make you a better employe? | 42% | 58% | 78% | 22% | 36% |
| Are your responsibilities generally well planned and organized? | 48% | 52% | 85% | 15% | 37% |
| **Leadership** | | | | | |
| Do you get cooperation from others when needed? | 82% | 18% | 90% | 10% | 8% |
| Does *teamwork* describe the company's organization? | 70% | 30% | 88% | 12% | 18% |
| Overall, is the company's treatment of people very fair? | 73% | 27% | 86% | 14% | 13% |
| Does ownership completely understand your work problems? | 42% | 58% | 73% | 27% | 31% |
| Do you feel updated as to what is happening in the company? | 55% | 45% | 79% | 21% | 24% |

*Continued on next page*

| | 2012 | | 2020 | | 20% or better |
| --- | --- | --- | --- | --- | --- |
| **Leadership cont.** | **Yes** | **No** | **Yes** | **No** | 85% or better |
| As an employee, do you feel you can trust your direct supervisor/manager? | 70% | 30% | 89% | 11% | 19% |
| **Performance** | | | | | |
| Do you understand completly what is expected in your job? | 85% | 15% | 96% | 4% | 11% |
| Do you get the help you need to do a good job? | 73% | 27% | 87% | 13% | 14% |
| Are the customers of the compnay pleased with the level of quality and service your company provides? | 76% | 24% | 97% | 3% | 21% |
| Does the compnay place a high priority on servicing its customers and developing customer loyalty? | 88% | 12% | 96% | 4% | 8% |
| **General** | | | | | |
| Does each department in this company have measurable standards designed to increase profitability? | 52% | 48% | 84% | 16% | 32% |
| Everything considered, is the compnay changing for the better? | 67% | 33% | 91% | 9% | 24% |

Continuous improvement like Trinity's builds autonomy. It says, in effect, that if you identify a problem, you're expected to bring it to the attention of your coworkers and management—and you may be asked to serve on a team to fix it. Employees learn that the workplace is theirs and that they can take responsibility for making it better. That's another way in which they come to think like businesspeople—like partners.

One more thing: In 2019 Trinity made another major stride toward employee engagement, ownership, and partnership culture. It became a 100 percent employee-owned enterprise, through an employee stock ownership plan, or ESOP. (I'll discuss the mechanics of ESOPs in chapter 5.) Now the company's employees are not just figurative owners or business partners; they are owners and partners.

Trinity's experience illustrates the essential elements of true empowerment, all made possible by the use of a key number. Understanding the business. Tracking and forecasting progress. Devising methods to make the number move in the right direction. There's just one more element of building partnership, as Trinity also discovered: making it worth everyone's while. Sharing the wealth that the partners create.

# 4

# PAYING THE PARTNERS

**SO FAR, WE** have looked at the key management ideas of the partnership system. Now let's look at what they mean for rank-and-file employees.

Implement these ideas and you are asking these folks to change the way they do things. You're asking them to learn what the key numbers mean, to track those numbers, and to forecast them. You're asking them to think up ideas to make the key numbers move in the right direction and then to implement those ideas.

You may also be speaking and acting a little differently yourself. Maybe you're using words like "partnership" and "trust" and "transparency." Hopefully, you are even more open and inclusive than you have been in the past. But you are also expecting people to take on more responsibility and to hold each other accountable for results.

All this is likely to be surprising and a little daunting for a lot of employees—and maybe for you as well. Some people will be resistant to change of any sort. Some will mistrust the whole thing. Many will simply be puzzled. They'll hold back and see what develops. And nearly everyone will be wondering, *What's in it for me?*

This last point—the time-honored question of human beings everywhere—is where a lot of change initiatives break down. The initiatives tell employees *what* they should do differently. They never explain *why* they should do things differently.

The partnership approach and the economic engagement it creates are different. Remember that the goal of this approach is to get employees thinking and acting like partners in the business so that they can improve results and their own work lives. Tracking the key number helps people understand the fundamental economics. Figuring out how to move the needle deepens that understanding. It gives your partners the experience of working together to help the company succeed. Right there is the ultimate "why" for anything they do.

But since business is an economic institution—its goal is to make money—partners have a right to share in the wealth they help build. They will want it. They will expect it. And if they are not fairly rewarded, they will naturally grow resentful, and rightly so. *Why should we work harder and smarter if all it does is put more money in somebody else's pocket? Just let me go back to doing my job!*

So this chapter is about how to reward your trusted partners effectively. It will look at sharing the economic wealth you and your partners are creating, and—the real key to progress—incentive plans. (The following chapter will examine employee stock ownership plans, or ESOPs, and other forms of equity sharing.) Incentive pay, often quite generous, is a central element of the whole system. Trouble is, too many companies get it wrong.

## PROFIT SHARING'S PROS AND CONS

Sharing a company's profits with employees—all the employees—has a long history in business. William Lever, founder of Lever Brothers (now Unilever), developed a scheme that provided his workers with a profit share amounting to 2–5 percent of their annual pay. William Cooper Procter, grandson of the cofounder of Procter & Gamble, introduced profit sharing at P&G as early as 1887. Then there was James Lincoln, who ran Lincoln Electric for many years before his death in 1965. Lincoln Electric, a global manufacturer of arc welding equipment, has long shared up to one-third of its annual profits with employees.[16] According to the company, the average bonus over the last decade amounts to 40 percent of an employee's base earnings.

Today, many companies, large and small, offer some sort of profit-sharing plan, though few are as generous as Lincoln Electric's. Southwest Airlines paid out $667 million in profit sharing in 2020, which added more than six weeks of extra pay (12.2 percent) to the typical employee's total compensation. About fifty thousand hourly workers at General Motors received $8,000 apiece in profit-sharing checks, also in 2020, while Ford workers got $6,600. Many of the smaller companies that have been my clients have profit-sharing plans in place. Perez Design Build Remodel, for instance, shares up to 30 percent of profits each year, depending on results.

Profit sharing can be an essential part of creating partners. It's often the mark of a company that truly values its people. It undoubtedly helps to build long-term loyalty and thus foster retention. But please understand: most profit-sharing plans are not *incentive* plans. Incentive plans, by definition, are supposed to affect people's behavior on the job, day in and day out. They encourage people to work harder and smarter, to go the extra mile, to collaborate with their coworkers, to come up with new ideas to improve some aspect of the business. They then reward people for doing all that.

A traditional profit-sharing plan doesn't have the same effect. How could it? At most companies, profit sharing is paid out once a year. It's management's decision how much to pay, or indeed whether to pay any at all. People rarely know what they must do to get the rewards, beyond doing a good job and getting along with the bosses. Many may not even understand how the company generates profits. When a profit-sharing check arrives, it means the business is doing well—all good. But it doesn't change the way the organization operates from day to day. It doesn't engage the employees in the economics of the company. If it helps a company increase its profits—the goal of most businesses—the effect is modest at best.

So now let's look at true incentive plans, often known to human resources (HR) professionals as gainsharing plans. I'll explain how they fit into the partnership system, how they reinforce economic engagement, and how they lead to better performance from one year to the next.

## INCENTIVE PLANS: WHAT NOT TO DO

First, let's examine some common mistakes in designing an incentive plan. I can't count the number of companies I have seen commit one or more of these four fundamental errors.

1. **The plan is based on individual rather than on team performance.** This is a big misstep. Business is almost always a team sport. Nobody wins unless everybody wins. Sales does not win if operations does not fulfill the order. Operations doesn't win if sales brings in orders that are not well suited to a company's capabilities. And then there's the problem of measurement. How accurately can you track individual performance in most jobs? Even when it's possible—in sales, for instance—individual bonuses send everyone the wrong message. A successful sales rep has doubtless

done a good job. But he or she couldn't have succeeded unless other departments were doing a great job too.

Make no mistake, I'm all in favor of rewarding individuals who are exceptionally talented or who regularly go the extra mile. But reward them with promotions, new opportunities, public recognition, and raises in base pay. Don't give them an incentive bonus. It tells everyone else that *they* don't have a rewardable impact on performance, and it discourages them from going the extra mile.

If you do try to measure individual performance in every job, you're opening up numerous cans of worms. Look at Lincoln Electric, which (oddly enough) does pay its profit-sharing bonuses based on individual performance. Factory workers get merit-based bonuses based on "output, quality, adaptability, dependability, teamwork, ideas, cooperation, and adherence to environmental, health, and safety standards," according to management professor James O'Toole, who has studied the company in depth. The metrics for white-collar employees include "customer focus, innovation, decision-making judgment, and working without supervision." Wow. How hard is it to differentiate every single individual along lines like these? "Managers at Lincoln," O'Toole acknowledges, "find determining fair and effective individual bonuses to be almost as complex and time-consuming as setting piecework rates; the process requires establishing meaningful, objective standards, then following up with rigorous data gathering and analysis."[17] Do you really want to get into all this? And do you want to have your managers spend a substantial fraction of their time evaluating every single individual's performance?

2. **The plan is imposed from the top, with no input from the troops.** If a company is big enough to have an HR department, the HR folks probably get the job of designing the plan. Otherwise, it's likely to be the company owner who takes it on. He or she will announce the plan with much fanfare.

   Really? How many initiatives handed down from above get instant buy-in and understanding? The sad part is this: If you involve employees in designing the plan, if you get their ideas about what matters most and what seems fair, then it's already their plan before it even launches. People will know what it's all about. They'll trust it.

3. **The plan is invisible**. You've probably seen it happen, maybe in your own company (though I hope not). The boss announces the plan at the beginning of the year and never mentions it again. At the end of the year, there may or may not be a bonus—who knows? Pretty soon people forget about the plan, at which point it has zero impact on how they do their jobs.

   The fourth pitfall is a little different, but in some ways it's the most important one to avoid:

4. **The plan isn't self-funding.** Companies get themselves into trouble on this one all the time. They tie a bonus to the attainment of individual goals, or perhaps to certain key performance indicators (KPIs). Guess what? People hit the goals! They knock the KPIs out of the park! Only trouble is, the company isn't doing so well. Cash is tight. Not a good time to pay a bonus . . . except we sort of have to, right?

   I *always* recommend that bonus plans be linked to key financial results, such as gross profit, or to indicators that have a direct and immediate effect on financial results, such as billable hours in an engineering firm. That way, you can be sure that hitting the targets will generate enough cash to pay the bonus, with some left over. An important test of the key number—and the foundation of a good incentive plan—is to examine the relationship between the key number and profit or cash in the last twelve months. The incentive plan should result in more money for everyone, company and employees alike.

## THE ALTERNATIVE: THE HIGHLY VISIBLE KEY-NUMBER INCENTIVE PLAN

By now you have probably figured out that a good incentive plan ties directly to the key number and that it needs to be up on the scoreboard where people can see it. Let me show you how it operates at one company I coached; then we'll go on to analyze what makes it work. Incidentally, I liked this company so much that I subsequently became an investor and now am the second-largest shareholder, after the founder.

The founder was Matt Plaskoff. Matt was already a leader in the construction industry when he came up with a new idea for a business. This one, he decided, would focus exclusively on remodeling bathrooms. It's one place where homeowners feel that they get a great deal of value for their money, so the business is less recession-sensitive than other construction and remodeling projects. The new business would also apply lean-manufacturing principles to bath remodeling. A bathroom that might take a typical remodeler three to five weeks would take Matt's new company only a week. Appropriately, he named the business One Week Bath.

The fledgling firm encountered some common entrepreneurial difficulties. It was undercapitalized in its early years, one reason Matt asked me to be both a business coach and an investor. He himself was shouldering most of the sales burden, and when he tried to hire more sales reps they didn't always work out. But soon things began to stabilize. With the usual inputs in hand, Matt and I developed a key-number system for the company, complete with scoreboard and meetings every Wednesday. We gave each of the project managers an internet-enabled tablet so they could attend.

The meetings begin at 8:12 a.m., not a minute sooner or later. First comes an update from sales, which provides a view of the company's backlog. If the backlog falls below eight weeks, everyone knows they have to focus on bringing in more business. If it's twelve weeks or more, the company may need to add a crew. After sales comes a report from the eleven project managers, telling where they stand on the key number: gross margin per day, broken down by job. All kinds of insights emerge from this process. One continuing challenge, for instance, was getting local building inspectors to show up on time. When the inspectors were a day or two late, the key number suffered. One of the project managers mentioned that he had begun calling the inspector to get on the schedule right at the start of each job. The other PMs immediately picked up on the idea, and now all the PMs call inspectors shortly after the start of a job. It's a simple improvement, but it worked. And it came right out of this process.

Another operating challenge—critical to a lean project-based company—was getting product ready for each of the jobs. The forecasting made it clear that the warehouse manager, who was responsible for this task, just wasn't up to it and needed a different position. A new hire—the daughter of the office manager, Bonnie—came on board. Her name was Krystal.

Now, warehouse manager is a tough job. It requires coordinating with hundreds of suppliers and designers. It involves staying in close touch with all the project managers and the sales staff to learn about upcoming projects. The goal is to have inventory ready for 100 percent of the scheduled projects two weeks in advance of the scheduled start of each job. At first, One Week Bath was running way south of 50 percent, which was killing our efficiency in the field. Krystal and her team began reporting every Tuesday afternoon, the day before the meeting, where we stood relative to the 100 percent goal. Slowly but steadily, the figure began to rise, driven by Krystal and her team, particularly purchasing. After several months, she announced that 100 percent of the next two weeks' jobs had product ready in the warehouse. Everyone cheered the announcement! She sort of had her own key number. But her efficiency had immediate effects on the company's key number because it increased everyone else's efficiency. Those effects were visible on the scoreboard.

The new warehouse management also made it possible for employees to do things they hadn't done before, as I discovered at one Wednesday meeting.

That day, there seemed to be a buzz in the air. We went through the sales update as always. Then someone announced that we had a new salesperson, Steve. I knew Steve as one of our project managers, so I asked him if he had changed jobs. "Not really, Bill," he said. "I just noticed that the home where we are remodeling three baths also had a fourth bath. The customer is really happy with our work, so I asked him if he would like us to take care of his fourth bath. The customer loved the idea. I got together with design and Krystal in the warehouse to see if we could get something pulled together in lightning fashion. Turns out we could! And so we have sold this bath and will have it installed while me and my crew are still there. By the way, our gross margin per day went up."

That's the way partners think. The other partners cheered.

## THE BONUS PLAN

Anyway, I promised to talk about One Week Bath's bonus plan. The first thing to note is that it's right up there on the scoreboard. The company's teams all see a weekly spreadsheet showing year-to-date net profit, the company's key number, as well as the central components of that figure, notably gross margin per day. They see the bonus they have earned so far, which is pegged to net profit. They also get a chance to see—and to add their views on—forecast profit and bonus for the remainder of the year. The thirty-minute Wednesday meetings update not only projected profits but also the projected bonus.

Here's an example. Figure 4.1 shows the numbers in the middle of one recent year. The bonus in the first quarter was twenty-nine hours of pay. The projected bonus in the second quarter was forty-one hours of pay, well above budget. Not surprisingly, this visibility gives employees an incentive to figure out how to make improvements. These are teams that pull together.

Note a few salient facts about this incentive plan. One, it's objective. It doesn't depend on some executive's assessment of performance. Two, it's wholly transparent. People know in advance what must happen in terms of profit levels for them to earn a bonus, and they know how big the bonus will be. Three, it's generous. If the company were to stay on track for this particular year, people would earn close to an extra seven weeks' worth of wages. Four, it's self-funding—that is, the increase in profits is substantially more than the cost of the bonus. This is a game worth playing for both owners and employees. Each week, as the scoreboard forecast goes up or down, so does the forecast bonus.

Figure 4.1

| Q1 Net Profit | Q1 Bonus in Paid Hours | Q2 YTD Net Profit | Q2 YTD Bonus in Paid Hours | Q3 YTD Net Profit | Q3 YTD Bonus in Paid Hours | Full Year Net Profit | Full Year Bonus in Paid Hours |
|---|---|---|---|---|---|---|---|
| $ 18,062 | 0 | $ 36,124 | 0 | $ 54,186 | 0 | $ 72,248 | 10 |
| $ 28,062 | 0 | $ 56,124 | 0 | $ 84,186 | 0 | $112,248 | 16 |
| $ 38,062 | 0 | $ 76,124 | 0 | $114,186 | 14 | $152,248 | 24 |
| $ 48,062 | 0 | $ 96,124 | 0 | $144,186 | 19 | $192,248 | 32 |
| $ 58,062 | 0 | $116,124 | 12 | $174,186 | 25 | $232,248 | 41 |
| $ 68,062 | 0 | $136,124 | 15 | $204,186 | 31 | $272,248 | 51 |
| $ 78,062 | 0 | $156,124 | 19 | $234,186 | 37 | $312,248 | 62 |
| $ 88,062 | 0 | $176,124 | 22 | $264,186 | 44 | $352,248 | 73 |
| $ 98,062 | 13 | $196,124 | 26 | $294,186 | 51 | $392,248 | 86 |
| $108,062 | 15 | $216,124 | 30 | $324,186 | 59 | $432,248 | 99 |
| $118,062 | 17 | $236,124 | 34 | $354,186 | 68 | $472,248 | 113 |
| $128,062 | 19 | $256,124 | 38 | $384,186 | 77 | $512,248 | 128 |
| $138,062 | 22 | $276,124 | 43 | $414,186 | 86 | $552,248 | 144 |
| $148,062 | 24 | $296,124 | 48 | $444,186 | 96 | $592,248 | 160 |
| $158,062 | 27 | $316,124 | 53 | $474,186 | 107 | $632,248 | 178 |
| $168,062 | 29 | $336,124 | 59 | $504,186 | 117 | $672,248 | 196 |
| $178,062 | 32 | $356,124 | 64 | $534,186 | 129 | $712,248 | 215 |
| $188,062 | 35 | $376,124 | 70 *41* | $564,186 | 141 | $752,248 | 235 |
| $198,062 | 38 | $396,124 | 77 | $594,186 | 153 | $792,248 | 255 |
| $208,062 | 42 | $416,124 | 83 | $624,186 | 166 *96* | $832,248 | 277 |
| $218,062 | 45 | $436,124 | 90 | $654,186 | 180 | $872,248 | 299 |
| $228,062 | 47 | $456,124 | 94 | $684,186 | 188 | $912,248 | 313 |

How do you create such a plan? It isn't hard. As the first few chapters pointed out, you have to work with your employees, managers, customers, and financial statements to define your company's issues. You have to define the key performance metric, and you have to begin tracking, broadcasting, and forecasting the company's results on this metric. Then you get together with people and take the following four steps:

1. Define the right group for the plan. In smaller companies—those with fewer than five hundred people—the right group is usually the whole staff. In larger ones, the key is to identify the appropriate team. It could be a branch or a functional unit, like Southwest's pilots. But be sure it includes everyone in that unit, support staff as well as frontline workers. Remember that business is a team sport.

2. Begin talking about the bonus plan with people in that group. By now they should understand the key number. Do they also begin to see how they can affect that key number? Do they understand the effects on company financial performance if it moves in the right direction? Ask what seems like a fair division of the incremental gains. This will give you a chance to explain that a profitable, growing company needs money to reinvest every year and that much of that money will have to come from profits. The owner or owners, of course, also are entitled to a continuing return on their investment and, in this case, on their involvement in the business.

3. Next, draft a plan. A handy rule of thumb is to distribute one-third of the incremental gains to employees in the form of a bonus while retaining two-thirds for the company. But every firm is different, and you will have to determine what's best in your own situation. Figure 4.2 shows one variation: a bonus in which the incentive pool increases with every incremental gain in financial performance. That can lead to a very generous bonus pool indeed!

4. Spell out the details. How much do we get and when do we get it? A few companies I have heard of pay everyone equally: they just divide up the bonus pool into same-size segments. But most companies I work with pay differential bonuses based on employees'

earnings, with everyone getting the same percentage of their base pay. (A few—SRC is one—pay managers a larger percentage of base pay because they have more responsibility.) Most make the payments every three months based on the quarter's performance. Some reserve a portion of the quarterly bonus pool until year-end to make sure the year's results justify a payout.

Finally, a good test of an incentive plan is to look at the pool of money in the plan at the end of the year and ask yourself this: If you were given the opportunity to buy an insurance policy the price of which was the incentive pool, and if you paid that premium only if you hit budget, would you buy that policy? The answer should be yes. If it is no, keep working on the plan.

Note that there is no cap on such a plan! Why should there be? Employees are free to earn as much in bonus as they possibly can because every dollar that goes into their pockets is matched (and then some) by the dollars going into the corporate coffers. Again, a true win-win situation. Partnership Principle #4 summarizes the main points:

**PARTNERSHIP PRINCIPLE #4**

Partners get a cut of the wealth they help create—and have a say in how big that cut is.

Some companies create this kind of incentive plan and then supplement it with a general broad-based profit-share check at the end of the year. To me, that's sort of redundant—they might as well just make the incentive plan more generous and thus more powerful. If they're worried about year-end results, they can withhold part of the quarterly payments. Otherwise, why wait?

Figure 4.2

## A bonus plan where the incentive pool increases as proft rises

| 2010 | 2011 | 2012 | 2013 | 2014 | 2015 Budget | |
|---|---|---|---|---|---|---|
| 3,793,436 | 4,372,958 | 4,288,616 | 4,211,374 | 8,029,225 | $11,044,000 | Revenue |
| 573,266 | 944,893 | 1,070,406 | 1,275,839 | 2,242,088 | $2,986,488 | Gross Profit |
| 15% | 22% | 25% | 30% | 28% | 26.0% | Gross Profit % |
| 556,061 | 758,518 | 899,978 | 1,404,276 | 1,989,826 | $2,150,000 | Operating Expenses |
| 17,205 | 186,375 | 170,428 | (128,437) | 252,262 | $1,067,586 | Net Profit |
| | | | | | $160,138 | Bonuses Paid |
| | | | | | 15.0% | Bonus Pool % of profit |

| Net Profit Before Taxes & Bonus | Gross Profit | Incentive Percent | Incentive Pool | Net Profit After Bonus | Bonus % of Employee Compensation | Bonus in Paid Hours |
|---|---|---|---|---|---|---|
| $100,000 | $100,000 | 1.00% | | | | |
| $267,568 | $2,186,488 | 7.00% | $18,731 | $248,855 | 0.99% | 20.5 |
| $367,568 | $2,286,488 | 8.00% | $29,407 | $338,179 | 1.55% | 32.2 |
| $467,568 | $2,386,488 | 9.00% | $42,083 | $425,504 | 2.21% | 46.1 |
| $567,568 | $2,486,488 | 10.00% | $56,759 | $510,828 | 2.99% | 62.1 |
| $667,568 | $2,586,488 | 11.00% | $73,434 | $594,152 | 3.86% | 80.4 |
| $767,568 | $2,686,488 | 12.00% | $92,110 | $675,476 | 4.85% | 100.8 |
| $867,568 | $2,786,488 | 13.00% | $112,786 | $754,800 | 5.94% | 123.5 |
| $967,568 | $2,886,488 | 14.00% | $135,462 | $832,124 | 7.13% | 148.3 |
| $1,067,568 | $2,986,488 | 15.00% | $160,138 | $907,448 | 8.43% | 175.3 |
| $1,167,568 | $3,086,488 | 16.00% | $186,814 | $980,773 | 9.83% | 204.5 |

## BONUS PLANS FOR LARGE COMPANIES

It's pretty easy to create a bonus for a small company. Big ones often find that corporate policies regarding compensation are an obstacle. But big companies are mostly just collections of small businesses, each with its own local economics. A large company that figures out how to pay bonuses based on a combination of unit and corporate performance—in a way that makes the whole thing objective, transparent, generous, and self-funding—will find that people soon come to understand the connection between performance and rewards. It will also find that they're motivated to do better, just as they are at One Week Bath.

A credit union I worked with, for example, already had a companywide annual profit-sharing program. But the company had many branches and decided to try the partnership approach in three of them. The question then came up: Do the test branches develop their own incentive plan or do they stay in the companywide profit-sharing plan? There was quite a discussion. Eventually, the company's leaders agreed to a cumulative quarterly incentive plan on incremental performance, starting at 5 percent above budget. The incentive plan for each member of the branch was determined 50 percent by local performance and 50 percent by the performance of all three test branches. The level of cooperation and joint accountability soared, as did the branches' performance.

One final word: it's often said that nobody works for money alone and that nobody is solely motivated by the prospect of more money. There's a lot of truth in that. If you're doing a job day in and day out, you may be motivated more by the demands of the work itself—the development of mastery, as bestselling author Daniel Pink puts it—and the people you're working with than by the prospect of financial gain. But people always like to win, and they like to feel that their efforts to help the company win are appreciated and rewarded. Nothing says "thank you" like several weeks' worth of extra pay. And nothing encourages people to think like partners as much as knowing they will be paid like partners—and knowing how they themselves contribute to larger and larger bonuses.

# 5

# OWNERSHIP:
# MAKING PARTNERSHIP LAST

**CONSIDER THE MAGIC** of the multiple.

As businesspeople and investors know, every dollar in incremental profit that a company earns adds three, five, maybe even ten or more dollars to the value of the company. Wall Street understands this link as the price-to-earnings ratio: if earnings rise, stock prices rise by a multiple of the earnings increase. But most financial folks just call it the multiple. Whatever you call it, it's the road to building long-term wealth.

Imagine, for instance, a successful entrepreneurial enterprise. Let's say it has been in business ten years and that it has grown steadily to $5 million in sales. Another ten years and it's up to $25 million, perhaps with a 10 percent post-tax return on sales. So its net profit is now $2.5 million. Depending on the industry, the company's growth prospects, and a dozen other factors, the business might be worth anywhere from $5 million to $25 million or more—a healthy asset by any standard, and one reason entrepreneurship continues to attract bright, ambitious people. This is what capitalism is all about.

So here's my view: if you really want people in your company to think and act like trusted partners—like businesspeople—you should consider sharing ownership. Owning a stake in a business is what turns people into capitalists.

Sharing ownership doesn't even have to be a sacrifice, because when people become owners they tend to work harder, work smarter, and do all they can to help grow the business. Hired hands don't care much about growth, but trusted partners do. "Giving up some ownership was the best thing I ever did," one company owner told us. "It's better to own fifty percent of a fifty-million-dollar business than a hundred percent of a ten-million-dollar business. Creating owners transforms the workplace."

Right now, I'd wager, the typical employee of the typical company doesn't understand much about the multiple and certainly doesn't feel like an owner. But there are plenty of ways to share ownership, and there are plenty of ways to bring home the long-term value of ownership and wealth creation. In fact, it's the logical conclusion of the kind of management I've been espousing in this book.

Some large companies, such as Procter & Gamble, sponsor employee stock purchase plans, which offer shares at a discount to the market price. Other publicly traded companies prefer distributing options or restricted shares—often just to a top tier of employees, but in some cases to the entire workforce. Starbucks provides so-called Bean Stock shares to all employees with a certain level of seniority. Technology companies have long operated on the assumption that they must provide equity in some form to their most talented employees; some extend the benefit to the entire workforce.

Privately held companies also have many options. The most common method is a government-approved employee stock ownership plan, or ESOP, which is a kind of trust held for the benefit of the employees.

I'll explain more about ESOPs later in the chapter; for now, all you need to know is that the shares held by the trust are allocated to individual employees over time. Of course, ESOPs aren't right for every company. Anthony Wilder Design/Build, a construction firm based in Maryland, considered an ESOP but decided against it due to cost and regulations. Instead, the company offers shares to employees for purchase, and the shares are valued using a multiple of earnings. Choice One Engineering, an Ohio company, did something similar and for similar reasons. TD Industries, a large mechanical contracting firm headquartered in Dallas, has created an ESOP; but unlike most ESOPs, it requires employees to buy into the plan through a payroll deduction. About 80 percent have done so, and the stock has risen steadily in the past several years.

## AN ESOP AT WORK

A typical ESOP is a little different. Let's take a look at Comfort Supply, a wholesaler of heating, ventilating, and air-conditioning (HVAC) equipment.

The company is headquartered in Nashville, Tennessee, and has seven other locations elsewhere in the state. Clay Blevins purchased the business back in 2002, when it had $3 million in sales, and has guided it along a successful path. In 2013 *Inc.* magazine named it one of the five hundred fastest-growing private companies in America. By 2019 it was doing roughly $32 million in sales.

In 2014, Blevins decided he wanted to share ownership in Comfort Supply with the people who had helped him build it. He was already running his company along the lines I have outlined in this book: partnership. His employees tracked and forecast key numbers. They shared in a quarterly bonus when times were good. They were beginning to think like businesspeople. One could say they were owners of the firm's short-term results. But Blevins wanted to get them to the next level, that is, owning the long-term results. According to government rules, shares held by an ESOP must be valued once a year by a professional appraiser. But Blevins didn't see how a once-a-year appraisal of the stock they now held would deepen their understanding or make them feel more like the owners they were.

So I worked with him to create a different approach: a scoreboard that showed the estimated value of the stock, based on a multiple of the company's past thirty-six months' worth of profits. It's a simple formula that allowed the company to update its valuation every week.

**Figure 5.1**

**Estimated share price at Comfort Supply**

**Share Price**

Figure 5.1 shows Comfort Supply's approximate share price valuation through the end of October 2015. It was open for all to see, so every employee knew both the past and current price. Not surprisingly, they quickly came to understand the reasons for the fluctuations. In early 2015, for instance, a major supplier experienced a quality problem that hurt Comfort Supply's sales and profits and thus the stock price. They could also see how well they responded to this challenge, generating sales and profits well above budget in the last several months of the year and driving the share price up.

But here's the real insight. Put yourself back at that moment in time—October, say. The chart shows the stock's actual valuation to the end of October, and it shows projected valuations for November and December. Like other partnership companies, Comfort Supply holds a weekly staff meeting at which managers forecast sales, costs, and profits, branch by branch, two to three months out. The meeting facilitates learning across all the branches as employees collectively try to improve their results. It also provides the data necessary to calculate a *projected* share price. Since the company has been forecasting profits as part of its management system for many years, the forecasts tend to be pretty accurate.

As you can see from the chart, employees' shares were worth an estimated thirty dollars per share in December 2014. In 2015, despite the challenges, it looked like the stock could hit close to forty dollars a share at year-end—about a 30 percent increase. Since the ESOP allocates shares to individual employees' accounts, each employee could calculate the value of his or her own shares and the future possibilities for wealth building if the share price continued to increase. They were beginning to learn the magic of the multiple.

Meanwhile, Blevins continued to engage his team more and more in running the business. At that point, for instance, team members were putting the final touches on the budget for 2016. But a budget is really just a twelve-month forecast. So once the numbers were firmed up, they could apply the valuation formula to estimate what their shares would be worth if they hit their budget targets—the multiple again. And of course, they would continue to track their progress as part of the weekly meeting.

It's this kind of nitty-gritty involvement in the business that makes ownership come alive. It comes in stages. If people don't understand how they can affect short-term results, it's premature to speak to them about driving long-term value. But once they come to see what they have to do to generate results, they can track the growth of their stake every month. It changes how people think and act.

Here's what Clay Blevins had to say about it: "There was an immediate, positive change in attitude here. Everyone learned more about business and earned more money. There has been very little turnover. Now employees are constantly bringing intelligent business ideas to the table. One of the best rewards is seeing someone who never had a shot at an education be able to show you how smart they really are. I have a warehouse worker with a GED who can tell me the current ratio of my business. I'm more proud of that than I am of anything else."

Thousands of privately held companies have created conventional ESOPs like Comfort Supply's. The ESOP may own anywhere from a minority of the shares to 100 percent. Many of these companies have a spectacular track record as employee-owned firms. Massachusetts-based Web Industries, for instance, used to be a small company in a low-margin industry, processing rolls of flexible material for industrial companies. Today it is a technologically sophisticated contract manufacturer that partners with world-class customers in health care, aerospace, and consumer health and hygiene. It has nine plants, and its global headcount is approaching eight hundred. Or take MSA Professional Services, which began life as a small civil-engineering firm in Baraboo, Wisconsin. Today it has sixteen locations around the country and more than three hundred engineers, architects, surveyors, environmental planners, and other specialists. Like Web, MSA is 100 percent owned by its employees.

## ESOP BENEFITS

A typical ESOP works like this: First, a company creates a formal trust. The trust is primarily funded either by the company itself or from a bank loan. If there's a loan—in this case it's known as a leveraged ESOP—the funds will be repaid from future company earnings, just as in a traditional leveraged buyout. The trust buys shares from the owner. Then, as the loan is paid down, the trust allocates shares to individual employees, usually based on a formula such as a percentage of annual compensation. (Government rules ban allocations that are too favorable to highly paid employees at the expense of others.)

So employees get their stock at no additional cost. It's a pure benefit, part of an employee's compensation for working, and its value is determined by the performance of the business. When people leave the company or retire, they sell the shares back to the company at the then-current appraised value. If the business is successful, they will have a nice nest egg for a comfortable retirement. But unlike other retirement plans—401(k)s, for example—the ESOP has the benefit of actually providing ownership. That helps people learn to think and act like trusted partners in the business while they're still working.

So selling your shares to an ESOP can help transform your company into a team of owners—of partners. Doing so provides company owners with other appealing benefits as well:

**Flexibility.** Although company owners often create ESOPs in anticipation of retirement, you can do it at any point in time. Regardless of when you set it up, you don't need to retire until you're ready to. Indeed, you can continue to run the company just as before—though I hope I have persuaded you to begin treating your co-owners as trusted partners rather than as hired hands.

**Legacy.** An ESOP-owned company stays independent. It perpetuates the founder's vision for the business and maybe his or her name as well. If you instead sell to a strategic buyer, who knows what will happen to the company—and to the people who helped you build it?

**Tax benefits.** An owner who sells at least 30 percent of the company's shares to the ESOP is allowed to defer payment of the capital gains tax he or she would owe on the transaction.

**A fair price.** Though strategic buyers may be prepared to pay a higher price, the ESOP is limited in what it can pay to the company's appraised value. However, tax and personal benefits may more than compensate for the price difference.

Some business advisors will tell you to stay away from ESOPs. You'll hear that they're too complex and too expensive. That can be the case for very small companies, but for a business of any size, it's nonsense. *Every* sale of a company, when done right, is complex and expensive. There's no way to avoid the lawyers, the lenders, and the accountants. And there are plenty of professionals who are highly knowledgeable about ESOPs. Of course, there's the occasional advisor who reveals his ignorance and prejudice with a dismissive "What, you want the inmates running the asylum?" Virtually all ESOP companies, of course, run exactly like conventionally owned businesses, complete with a board and a CEO. And no, they don't think of their employees as inmates.

The real payoff of sale to an ESOP may be the opportunities it opens for companies to thrive and grow. And why shouldn't they? Thanks to favorable legislation, many ESOP companies pay little or nothing in corporate income tax, so they have more cash available for investment. The employees are likely to be more engaged in their work, more knowledgeable about the business, and more committed to helping the company succeed. After all, it's theirs.

It's important to note that giving employees equity doesn't automatically change people's attitudes and behaviors. A true culture of ownership, one that encourages everyone to take their ownership seriously and act accordingly, depends on participative management. When I worked with Ameritech in the early 2000s, all the employees owned some stock in the company. But you couldn't find a real owner in the place. Research has consistently shown that significant improvement in company performance comes from the *combination* of shared ownership and participative management—or as I would refer to it, a company of trusted partners. Here's the fifth principle:

## PARTNERSHIP PRINCIPLE #5

Partners think long term, like owners.

## OTHER TYPES OF OWNERSHIP

Some companies are too new or too small for an ESOP. And some company owners resist the idea of sharing equity broadly. Maybe it doesn't feel right. Maybe they would prefer to pass the entire business on to their heirs. There are plenty of reasons for hesitation. But even in those situations, there are useful methods for bestowing the benefits of ownership on your employees and thereby helping them become trusted partners. The methods go under names such as phantom equity, stock appreciation rights, and the like. The idea is simple: no equity actually changes hands, but employees receive a certain number of "phantom" shares and then earn payouts pegged to the value of real shares in the business. Because this isn't a government-regulated plan like the ESOP, a company can structure the program pretty much how it wants to.

Here's how it worked at one company.

Sy Israel founded Universal Engineering Sciences (UES), headquartered in Florida, back in 1966. I met Sy and his son Mark at a conference in 2002, and we hit it off. They seemed to think that the pragmatic, principled ideas of economic engagement and partnership made a lot of sense. They wanted to try applying these practices in their business.

The company's business was environmental testing, typically for commercial enterprises that were building new locations. Like most entrepreneurial companies, UES had had its ups and downs. Sales and profits rose steadily between 1966 and 1999. But the three years after 1999 brought stagnating sales and falling profits, to the point where earnings in 2002 were less than half of 1999's.

So after performing the usual diagnostic process, UES chose to focus on profits, broken down by each of the eleven branches it had at the time. Each week via conference call, every branch would report its results. It would also forecast the next month's sales and profits, comparing the forecast to budget. Eventually this process expanded into a three-month rolling forecast. If there were changes in the past week's forecast, someone would need to explain the reasons.

Since all the branches were in the same business, that led to a great deal of collective learning. One manager noted the importance of diversifying his customer base and keeping up a continuing hunt for hard-to-find talent. Another wrote to himself, "Don't be afraid to test the pricing limits for services." The branches learned from each other and also competed to see who could show the best sales growth and profitability. Soon, business results were on the way up.

By 2004, things were on a roll: the company was headed toward a record level of sales and profits. But stuff happens. Hurricane Charley hit Punta Gorda, Florida, the morning of August 13 of that year. Many in the southwestern part of the state had expected to watch the storm pass by. It didn't. The following Monday, UES got word that the roof of the Punta Gorda office was gone. Mark Israel promptly excused that group from the meeting—but the Punta Gorda people stayed on. Most jobs were on hold, they pointed out, but the Federal Emergency Management Agency (FEMA) badly needed technical people with trucks and equipment, and the pay was good. Suddenly Punta Gorda had become a different kind of profit center!

So 2004 set record sales and profits after all. In the spring of the next year, Mark called me to discuss an equity program for the company, particularly the managers. I suggested looking into an ESOP, particularly given the tax advantages provided to the selling owners, and gave him some contacts. But after doing the research, he told me he didn't like the idea. He felt an ESOP was too expensive and complex for his company. More important, he was uncomfortable with sharing equity broadly—he wanted to limit the program to the company's branch managers, who in many ways were its key personnel. He asked if I would be willing to work with him on such a program.

So that's what we did. I first looked at the valuations of the few public companies in UES' industry, understanding that this firm's value would be discounted because of its relatively small size and lack of public-market liquidity. We then developed a simple valuation based on trailing three-year earnings, much like the method at Comfort Supply. Mark liked the approach because managers could easily see how their work drove the value of the stock as well as their quarterly bonuses. And we could update the value of the stock every month when the monthly financials were prepared.

Funding the program turned out to be easy. Mark had started a re-tirement program for the managers a few years earlier. Now he would let them choose whether they wanted to transfer those funds into UES eq-uity or leave them in the existing program. Ironically, the biggest single challenge turned out to be getting the company's lawyer to put together a legal agreement for the plan. The lawyer had initially been opposed to any equity agreement and agreed to it only when Mark explained that this was just an evolution of the company's existing retirement program.

We also made certain to call the equity interest shadow stock. The managers would not be formal stockholders with voting control; rather, they would own a financial interest in the value of company shares.

The company rolled out what came to be called the Capital Appre-ciation Plan at a subsequent meeting of the managers. Like stock ana-lysts, Mark and I presented the branch managers with the fifteen-year history of UES, which had averaged growth of 15 percent per year. The bullet-point outline of the estimated value of the retirement of a thirty-year-old manager looked something like this:

- Company contributes $2,000 per year
  - Funds grow at the same rate as UES' company value
  - Value cannot fall below $2,000 per year contribution
  - Retire at age 65
  - Question: What is the value of your UES-funded retirement?
  - Answer: It depends on the profit growth of UES . . .
  - What is the minimum value at retirement?
  - Answer: $70,000

There followed a discussion about what the future growth of the company would be versus the 15 percent historic growth. It was an interesting conversation, covering new branches, challenges with finding good staff, the benefits of UES' growing positive reputation, and so on. The managers' estimates of potential annual growth ranged between 7 and 20 percent. We then looked at the valuation implications depending on the rate of future growth, in the form of the table (Figure 5.2).

**Figure 5.2**

**Potential growth of a nest egg at UES**

| Growth | Retirement |
|--------|-----------|
| 0% | $ 73,525 |
| 2% | $ 106,879 |
| 4% | $ 159,202 |
| 6% | $ 241,857 |
| 8% | $ 372,973 |
| 10% | $ 581,339 |
| 12% | $ 912,461 |
| 14% | $ 1,437,905 |
| 16% | $ 2,269,609 |
| 18% | $ 3,581,690 |
| 20% | $ 5,643,471 |

We made it clear that anyone who left the company prior to retirement would forfeit their shadow stock at a 20 percent discount to the value at the date they left, and would be paid either cash or a five-year note to avoid a cash crunch. We asked if there were any questions. Most wanted to know when they could start. But then, as the conversation died down and I thought we were about to end the meeting, one of the managers stood up and said something like this: "I have always loved working at UES and really appreciated the bonus program we started in 2002. But this stock program is more than I ever dreamed of. I can see how I can take care of my long-term future and retirement, doing the things I love to do at UES. Mark and Sy, I just wanted to tell you how much this meant to me."

By the time I started to write this chapter, Universal had grown into a 750-plus-person, eighteen-branch operation. It had been named a National Top 500 Design Firm by *Engineering News-Record* every year since 1985. It was the largest family-owned firm of its kind in the United States. But then, at the end of May 2020, I got a call from Mark. I had not spoken with him in more than ten years. I asked why he was calling.

"You cost me four million!" he exclaimed.

I was nonplused. "Really! Um, how did I do that?"

"Do you remember that capital appreciation program you helped us set up?" Mark asked.

I said sure.

"Well," he continued, "we recently sold eighty percent of the company to a private equity firm for more than I ever imagined, and I just tallied all the capital appreciation plan payouts. They came to just over four million dollars."

"Great news!" I said. I didn't mind costing him the $4 million at all.

But Mark wasn't finished. "Let me tell you what was really great. One of our managers, a terrific guy who has been with us forever, got a payout of four hundred thousand dollars. When I gave him the check he looked at me and said, 'I have never seen that much money in one place, let alone in my hand. My financial future is secure, and I want to let you know how much I appreciate that.'"

Mark went on to explain that the value of the company had jumped 40 percent in the last year, and some of the managers did not want to sell their shares. Given the nature of the Capital Appreciation Plan, they did not have the option to hold on to them. But as one manager put it, "I don't see anything I could invest in that would have a reasonable chance at forty percent growth in a year." He understood the magic of the multiple.

Mark and Sy had transformed their company. They had transformed their managers from hired hands into trusted partners. They "finished big," as Bo Burlingham puts it in his book of that name—and they made sure their partners finished big with them.[18]

# 6

## WHAT HAPPENS TO
## PARTNERSHIP IN A CRISIS?

**AS YOU MAY** have guessed by now, "partnership" does not refer to some sort of good-hearted-but-soft-headed style of management. It is not a touchy-feely "kumbaya" approach to running a business. Rather, it is a disciplined business system that relies on transparency, economic understanding, respect, and mutual accountability. The engagement that it fosters is real engagement, involving both the head and the heart.

So running a business in this fashion is not necessarily easy. It is particularly challenging when something or someone, either outside or inside the company, seems bent on undermining it. And since those somethings or someones are always with us in one form or another, we better talk about how you can handle them. This chapter examines external crises, while the following chapter looks at what happens when people somehow undermine partnership from within.

### PANDEMICS AND OTHER CATASTROPHES

The COVID-19 pandemic of 2020 was just about the worst business crisis that most of us ever experienced. For months, the economy fell off a cliff. Unemployment skyrocketed. Some industries shut down completely. Others scrambled to keep up with unexpected demand, even while coping with supply-chain interruptions and sickness among employees.

But the pandemic is hardly alone in its disruption of twenty-first-century business as usual. There was 9/11, back in 2001. There was the financial crisis and sharp recession of 2008–2009. There have been catastrophic weather events, including tornados, fierce hurricanes, and out-of-control wildfires. The foreseeable future is likely to hold more of the same. What are the lessons for businesspeople?

One lesson is what not to do: instant and wholesale layoffs the minute a crisis hits.

Ironic, isn't it? Companies like to use the language of partnership and point to employees as "trusted partners." They say that their people are their most important assets. And then, when the company faces difficulties, they promptly let everyone go.

So much for partnership.

Boeing, for example, laid off 10 percent of its workforce during the first few months of the pandemic. But it was hardly alone. Companies large and small engaged in wholesale layoffs as the crisis worsened. Some 93 percent of restaurant employees were laid off at the lowest point.

Compare that approach with how Southwest Airlines responded to previous crises, both 9/11 and the recession. In both cases, the effect on airlines was devastating. Some wound up in bankruptcy court. All furloughed many of their employees. Except Southwest.

Around 2008, I traveled to Dallas, Southwest's home base. The local television station ran a story on how Southwest was bucking the industry trend by not laying anyone off. When I checked in on a Southwest flight later that day, I mentioned the story to the gate agent. "Great press," I said, and complimented her on the company's approach.

She replied, "Would you like to know *why* we're not laying anyone off?"

I said I would.

"Well, this is a bad time, for sure. Our whole country is hurting. But you know what? Sooner or later there are always downturns. The other airlines are loaded up with debt, so they have no choices. We have more than a billion in cash, so we have all kinds of options. In fact, we're going to be opening up some new cities."

It wasn't just Southwest's balance sheet that helped the airline prepare. A program dubbed Plane Smart Business, launched shortly before the crisis hit, helped employees understand the economics of the business and how they could improve the company's performance. So the employees were already trusted partners—and the company treated them as such.

Southwest, I should note, is not unique among large companies. Herman Miller, the furniture maker, declined to lay off any employees during the severe recession of the early 1980s. Lincoln Electric has never laid anybody off. Think of what it would be like to work at one of these companies, where layoffs are a last resort, not the first response. What sense of security would you enjoy? What level of commitment would you have? How envious would you be if you worked for a competitor? Companies like these become the employers of choice in their industry, which means they get the best and the brightest. And they get the real team players. It's no wonder that these companies have stock performance consistent with their industry leadership. I should know—I've been a Southwest shareholder for over forty years.

But what about smaller companies? Surely they have to lay off people, right? They can't possibly afford to keep everyone on the payroll when business dries up. Well, many of my clients—partnership companies all—would beg to differ. So would plenty of other entrepreneurs and business owners.

Take Canlis, a family-owned restaurant that has long been one of Seattle's iconic fine-dining restaurants. As the pandemic picked up speed, states began issuing orders for companies to close and people to stay home. Canlis's traditional business dried up in a heartbeat.

But owners Mark and Brian Canlis convened their team and came up with three new ideas. One was a morning business focused on bagels and coffee. Another was a drive-up burger service, which would allow the restaurant to get some use out of its aged-beef inventory. The third was takeout fine dining, with servers taking on the role of deliverers. As it happened, the bagel business couldn't cope with demand; the bagels sold out quickly, and drivers who had waited in line to get theirs were annoyed. The burger service, too, was a little too popular: it provoked complaints of big traffic tie-ups. Both offerings had to be discontinued. But the dinner service boomed, and the company was able to keep all of its 115 employees on the payroll, preparing and delivering exquisite meals that kept the Canlis name alive.

My colleague Henry Patterson, a restaurant consultant, asked Mark Canlis whether he ever considered laying people off. The response: "No. Why would I?"

Another example is Dan Price, CEO of Gravity Payments, also based in Seattle. In 2015, Price got a lot of publicity—not all of it favorable, by any means—when he raised his company's minimum salary to $70,000 a year. For the following five years, Gravity thrived.[19] But in 2020, the COVID-19 pandemic led to a more than 50 percent drop in revenue, and Gravity was facing possible bankruptcy in a period of months. So Price met with all of his company's employees in small groups, made sure they understood the financial situation, and asked for ideas. Pretty soon, everyone had agreed to a pay cut, with higher-paid employees taking the biggest hit. "Instead of underestimating your people, trust them," wrote Justin Bariso in an *Inc.* magazine article on Gravity. "The more information you can provide, the better they'll understand the situation and be willing to help."[20]

That reminded me of what Anthony Wilder Design/Build did during the earlier financial crisis. There, too, the owners presented the company's full financial situation to the employees. There, too, everyone agreed to pay cuts. Owners Anthony and Liz Wilder reduced their pay by 50 percent. Managers took a 30 percent hit, and the rest of the staff 20 percent.[§]

## BE PREPARED FOR THE UNEXPECTED

Approaching major crises with a spirit of teamwork and partnership requires two things. One is a strong balance sheet. You can't easily cope with an emergency if you haven't anticipated the possibility that there might someday be an emergency. Years ago people talked about putting money aside for a rainy day. It's still a good idea, and one that should come naturally if you have genuine concern for the well-being of all the partners in your business.

The other is a high level of economic knowledge on the part of the workforce and a willingness on the part of management to consult them. If your workforce does not understand your business's economics, their ability to help is limited. And even if employees are willing, they need to be told what to do, limiting your resources and ability to react quickly.

---

§   You can see a news report on this at https://www.youtube.com/watch?v=54XFM-ElhyPQ&feature=.

But a company of partners can move quickly and nimbly. Others call this making your business more agile. I agree.

Adams + Beasley Associates (ABA—we met them in chapter 1) is a company that had both a strong balance sheet and a high level of economic understanding. When the pandemic hit, ABA staff had already been tracking their job-security index for eleven months. The index was a combination of anticipated gross margin from the company's backlog plus cash in the bank. Like gross margin, it was updated every week. The pandemic put nearly all of the backlog on hold, and the flow of leads slowed to a trickle. But the company still had five months' worth of cash, and it had a group of trusted partners in its employees. So what could be done? In a few days, over a hundred ideas poured in. Several employees, stuck working from home, said they would call current and past clients to see how they were doing and ask what help they might need when the shutdown ended. Others installed a new information system to process invoices more efficiently. Still others cleaned and organized the millwork shop, readying tools for new projects. The company began devoting its weekly meetings to prioritizing and maintaining traction on these ideas and others.

Unusual? Unfortunately, yes. One ABA project manager said he had spoken to his counterpart in a competitor's shop. "We have no idea what is going on," complained his friend. "Five people were fired last week. We're guessing there will be more layoffs this week. By the way, let me know if you have any openings."

FAE, the engineering firm I wrote about in chapter 3, found itself in a similar situation. It had racked up record revenues in 2019. January and February 2020 topped 2019's performance. The company's backlog was well above $1 million, indicating a need to add staff. And then came the pandemic. By the end of March, the proposal backlog had dropped by 70 percent. Even committed projects were being canceled. The staff was scared. But after the initial shock, the people at FAE began thinking of the situation not just as a catastrophe, though it was certainly that, but also as an opportunity. The best companies in any industry, they realized, would survive and likely prosper when the crisis was over. If things got really tough, there would be salary reductions. But at no time were layoffs considered. You don't lay off partners.

So they doubled down on customer outreach. They kept an eye out for competitors that were closing their doors, realizing that those firms' customers might be in the market for engineering services. They drew up a list of responsibilities for drafters and for engineers, and they developed a list of ideas from every member of the team. Drafters were primarily responsible for finding contact information of prospective clients. Engineers were responsible for calling these prospects. Each week the staff would review their progress, reporting out individual by individual the number of billable hours and what each person had done to help the company's situation. They shared lessons learned, such as what led to the most-effective calls or what voicemail message was most effective.

Katie, the office manager, created a performance-tracking chart so everyone could see how they were doing in developing contacts, making calls, generating proposals, and subsequently winning new work, both by individual and across the entire team. Several weeks in, it became clear that the drafters had generated more contacts than the engineers could keep up with. So several drafters joined the engineers in making calls, after sitting in on a role-played meeting led by the most effective engineer caller. Remember, FAE is not a telemarketer; it is an engineering firm. Most team members were not particularly comfortable in a sales-and-marketing role. But in the face of the crisis, the focus among the trusted partners was simply to do what was needed to succeed. In doing so, they developed skills that would serve them well when the crisis abated. The sixth principle:

**PARTNERSHIP PRINCIPLE #6**

Partners face adversity together.

## MANAGING THE UPS AND DOWNS OF BUSINESS

Disruptions on the order of 9/11 and the pandemic have been relatively rare. We can only hope they stay that way. Other big events, like the 2008 financial crisis or weather-related catastrophes, are more common though still infrequent. But every business faces the possibility of what we might call ordinary crises. These are disruptions caused by the vagaries of business itself. A big customer suddenly decides to quit buying from you. A new, well-funded competitor enters your market. Technology changes, and you must quickly adapt your business model. The list goes on and on, and nearly every business owner I know has examples to add.

Take Kinko's, for instance. If you're a millennial or younger, you may not recognize the name; Kinko's was bought in 2004 by Federal Express and now operates under the FedEx Office brand. But Kinko's copy shops were once familiar sights in the nation's cities and college towns, and Kinko's was a great entrepreneurial success story.

The founder was Paul Orfalea, and the date was 1970. Back then, there were no personal computers. College students had to type their term papers and theses on manual or electric typewriters. Then they had to take the papers to a copy shop so they would have a backup. The copying machines made by Xerox and its competitors were big, expensive, and often cranky. Students might have to pay ten cents or more a page—a rate that could add up to a lot of money in those days—and wait a long time to get their copies. Kinko's—the name came from Orfalea's own nickname, reflecting his kinky red hair—offered quick, cheap copying. It was open twenty-four hours a day. It sold a variety of office supplies as well as copying services. For a bleary-eyed college student completing a paper at two o'clock in the morning, it was a godsend. The slogan was, "Go to Kinko's for your copies."

The business thrived, and soon Orfalea was considering how to expand. Instead of franchising, he set up partnerships with local entrepreneurs. Each store would be independently owned and operated, but it would license the Kinko's name and follow the Kinko's model. Within a decade there were eighty stores around the country. (The company's reach eventually extended to twelve hundred locations and twenty-three thousand employees in ten countries.) It expanded into downtown locations, serving business customers who needed quick, inexpensive copying. All locations were partnerships between Paul and the local owner.

Then came a potential crisis. The internet was still a long way away, but many companies had begun linking their facilities through proprietary networks. Business customers might want several copies of a proposal in three different locations—say, Houston, Chicago, and Las Vegas. If Kinko's couldn't offer this service, a competitor certainly would, and soon. Orfalea's team developed a network called Kinkonet and began talking to the entrepreneurs who ran Kinko's stores about installing and using the network.

But that's where they ran into problems. Each location was fiercely independent. "Retail is detail," was the mantra. Nobody really thought of themselves as part of a Kinko's network.

My colleagues and I worked with Kinko's to figure out what to do, applying the same partnership principles. Fortunately, Orfalea had long recognized the importance of sharing information and profits with his employees. He encouraged all of his local partners to operate in the same way. So the level of economic engagement at most Kinko's locations was high. In reviewing the network opportunity with Orfalea's team, it became clear to us that the new network service would support higher margins and generate a lot of repeat business. So the only question was how to get all the locations to appreciate the opportunity and act as a network when required.

The solution they developed with our help was pretty simple. We provided every outlet with detailed instructions about how Kinkonet worked, so that it wouldn't seem scary or difficult. More important, we developed an economic model that made sense to everybody. According to the plan, 25 percent of the revenue from a network job would go to whatever location got the initial order. The balance of 75 percent would be split among all the other locations that supported the order. So if there were five locations involved, each would get 15 percent of the revenue. This way, each location was independently responsible for its costs and efficiencies, which the location itself controlled. But all the locations could add revenue from business that originated elsewhere, with very little additional cost. When we shared an example of a typical order, the owners could see how profitable the service could be for everyone. Soon more and more outlets were signing on to Kinkonet, and the business soared. Kinko's stayed well ahead of any competitive service.

Incidentally, Kinko's never sacrificed anything in terms of the retail business. Retail was still detail. But the network business was built on top of the retail. Since business users typically discussed a job in the back office with the outlet's manager, the new slogan became, "Retail is detail, but the back door is worth more." Orfalea built a business on entrepreneurship, a commitment to employees, and economic engagement. All three enabled his organization to take a potential technology threat and turn it into an opportunity.

## THE CASH CRUNCH OF GROWTH

For fast-growing entrepreneurial companies, one of the most common "ordinary" crises is simple: not enough cash. It's a problem that inexperienced company builders rarely anticipate. When their companies begin to grow and make money, they think, "Terrific! We're on our way." Then they find that there isn't any cash in the bank.

How can this be? Well, growth requires investment. You hire more people. You open up new locations. You offer new products or services. All that takes money, right now. The payoff will come somewhere down the line. So unless your base business is extraordinarily profitable, you will likely not have enough cash to finance the growth. If this is the case, there won't be any "down the line."

This is a problem that an entrepreneur I'll call Henry Robinson ran into with his company. (The real entrepreneur has requested anonymity, so I have changed a few details about the company to protect privacy.) It happens all the time to entrepreneurs like Henry, who think of themselves more as human-services professionals or engineers or anything other than a businessperson.

A healthcare clinician, Henry had founded the company to offer wellness services. Its customers were companies that offered these services to their employees as a benefit. The selling proposition was simple: if your employees are healthier and happier, that's a good thing in itself; it will help those employees become more productive; and it will reduce turnover, which will help drive profitable growth. Henry's company grew slowly but steadily.

But as it grew, he and his team faced three problems. One was that it required more and more cash for working capital. Henry had originally funded the company with an investment. Over time, he had given the company more and more money in the form of loans. But eventually he was tapped out. A second issue: Henry enjoyed the care side of the business but disliked the management side. Yet management increasingly claimed more of his time.

The third concern was more an opportunity than a problem: the company saw a chance to offer its services to colleges and universities. It had been referred to academic institutions by some of its business clients, and the academic market looked like a high-growth opportunity. If Henry and his team didn't grab it, a competitor would. But this just added to the two other challenges.

Henry tried hiring executives to run things. One, a finance pro, worked out well, but another never earned the respect of the company's clinicians, its key employees. Henry came to the conclusion that that individual was not a good fit. He then took the situation to his board, explaining that he was at a point of personal crisis. One of the board members suggested he get in touch with me.

Henry and I got together a few weeks later and discussed the principles of economic engagement and building trusted partners. He was receptive to the idea, but skeptical. "Our staff are mostly clinicians," he told me. "They like helping people. They aren't very interested in business." But he decided to proceed, and we gathered the usual information from employees, managers, customers, and the financial statements. The process revealed a lot about the company. Customers raved about the services the company provided. Employees and managers spoke of the passion they had for providing good care and making a difference in people's lives. But then there were the financials, which no one but Henry and the finance guy ever saw. The financials showed steady growth with thin margins, requiring more and more cash from Henry.

At that point we pulled together a meeting of ten people, including Henry and the finance executive plus several other team members, mostly nurses. After reviewing the data, I asked the team members to answer a few questions:

- What would indicate that this company is *winning* in the coming year? Everyone agreed that the company's primary purpose was to serve people and change their lives. The more lives they touched, the more the company was winning.

- Then I asked what we needed to do to improve more lives. The team members knew there was a lot of demand for the company's services. So they needed to hire more clinicians.

- And what was stopping the company from hiring more clinicians? Some suggested that it was tough to find good people, but most of the group felt that the recruitment problem was manageable. The real problem was that Henry wouldn't let them hire more people.

- Why was Henry reluctant to hire more clinicians? We put this question to him directly. He explained that he had put every dime he had into the company. He couldn't put in anymore, and the company wasn't generating any extra cash. So adding more staff wasn't an option.

- The final question to the group was this: Are you serious about serving more patients and changing more lives? If so, you need to come up with ways for the company to become more profitable so it can generate the cash it needs to grow.

Henry sighed with relief. Suddenly he wasn't the only one who was thinking about how to become more profitable. He had partners to help carry the load. The group discussed the options and came up with the idea of a scoreboard that tracked revenue per clinician. If this number rose, the company's profitability would increase as well. The increased profit would generate the cash needed for expansion.

Soon everyone at the company was tracking this key number. The team updated the scoreboard each week and learned to forecast the number. Team members came up with a variety of ideas, such as scheduling appointments more efficiently and offering new services based on patient requests. And sure enough, revenue per clinician began to rise, as did profits and cash. Henry began hiring more clinicians and paying off some of the company's debts. The cash crisis was a turning point for his company, thanks to his ability to turn employees into trusted partners.

## SURVIVING—AND THRIVING

A crisis, so it is said, brings out the best and the worst in people. It brings out the best and the worst in companies too. Facing acute difficulties, some companies seem to panic. Some desperately try to cut costs, laying off people right and left. Others cling resolutely to business as usual, hoping against hope that whatever is causing the problem will disappear.

But then there are companies that not only survive the challenge but wind up thriving. If you step back from all the examples, you can see three things that all of them have in common.

1.  **They view their employees as assets, not liabilities.** They count on those employees not just to pitch in but to come up with innovative ideas both to adapt to the crisis and to take advantage of new opportunities. They understand that good ideas come only

from people, and the people most likely to come up with good ideas are the people working in the business. Canlis's people came up with three solutions to the pandemic crisis. Only one of these panned out—but that one kept the company alive. The ideas from Henry Robinson's team helped turn the company around.

2. **Company leaders and employees alike understand the economics of the business.** That's how Kinko's was able to get people signed on to the new network so quickly, just by making the economics transparent. And it's no accident that the Southwest gate attendant understood why her company wasn't laying off anybody—Southwest makes a point of making sure its workers know the airline's economics.

3. **These companies see themselves as more like a family than a conventional company.** Back when nearly all companies and farms were family businesses, nobody got laid off, because you can't lay off a family member. So the family's leaders had to ensure that they had enough resources set aside for a downturn. In modern terms, they maintained strong balance sheets. To companies like Southwest, ABA, and the others, layoffs aren't a tactic. They are an admission of failure.

To be sure, no company can keep going if its revenue dries up for too long or if it runs out of cash. But crises can be faced head-on. A partnership company with a committed team is in the best position not just to survive but to thrive.

# 7

# UNDERMINING PARTNERSHIP FROM WITHIN

**NOW LET'S LOOK** at a different kind of challenge: the internal kind.

Internal business challenges come in many forms. For example, maybe there are a handful of employees who shouldn't have been hired in the first place. They're perpetually late, often absent. They do the minimum amount of work. They badmouth the company every chance they get. Jim Collins was right when he said the first step toward a successful company is to get the right people on the bus. In this case, there's often no solution except to let them go. When you do, you usually find that the other employees are grateful. "Finally you got rid of the bad apples!"

But sometimes, something more challenging is going on. Maybe people are stealing from the company. Maybe there's a union with a history of opposing every managerial initiative, to the point where hourly workers and managers no longer trust one another. I've seen all sorts of conflict-ridden situation in my years as a business coach. I've also seen how the partnership principles can frequently overcome the difficulties.

## EMPLOYEE THEFT

Let's start with an all-too-common problem: employee theft. Another of my Australian clients had to face that one head-on.

Post Form Laminating has been a pioneer in the fabrication of laminate bench tops and countertops in Queensland. The business is owned and operated by David and Prue Pring, who are its president and office manager respectively. The pair are passionate advocates of lean and continuous improvement principles, which have helped the company reduce production lead-times while still providing high levels of quality and customer service. I met David and Prue in 2008, when I was working with BHP. But it wasn't until 2014 that I got another call from David.

At that point, he said, his business was struggling. Stone countertops were gaining popularity, reducing demand for laminate. I asked him to send me the last few years of financial statements, just to get a sense of how dire their situation was. And indeed, it was pretty rough. The company had no meaningful amount of equity on the balance sheet. Most of the debt that was supporting it came from loans from David and Prue. The market prospects were challenging, given the evolution of customer tastes away from laminate.

So we went through the process outlined in this book. The input from employees, managers, financials, and customers led to a key number: throughput per total paid hours. Throughput was calculated as revenue minus material expense, which was typically 40 percent of revenue. Once we confirmed that this ratio was a good predictor of profitability, we put together a scoreboard and an incentive plan. Though the number was readily understood by the team, the early going was tough. But employees now had a stake in improved performance, and gradually both throughput per paid hour and profits began to increase. Bonus payments increased as well—an anomaly in this industry.

But then, in 2018, with things looking up, something happened that caught David and Prue wholly by surprise.

It started with a discrepancy in the petty cash account. Initially the owners felt it was just an accounting error. But more discrepancies appeared. When money vanished from the petty cash drawer on a Saturday, David and Prue were sure something untoward was going on. And since only two individuals had access to the office and petty cash, it didn't take long for them to figure out who the culprit was. The thief was a manager, one of the few on the payroll. I'll call him George.

David and Prue felt betrayed, particularly in light of all the company had gone through. Fortunately, their accounting systems had alerted them to the problem; but now they had to determine what to do. Their initial inclination was to report George to the police and file charges. But after thinking it through, they decided to get more information. They knew George had not been doing a great job over the past several months. Further investigation revealed that he had a serious drinking problem and marital issues as well.

For years David had thought of George as a key player, and for years he was. So David decided to have a private meeting with him to discuss both the theft and the drinking problem, as they were clearly related. At first, George denied both. However, when confronted with the evidence, he became emotional and deeply ashamed. After resigning, he really hit rock bottom, winding up hospitalized in an intensive care unit, with acute health issues. He has since turned his life around and is employed in a different industry, but the damage to his family and reputation was in many ways irreparable.

David and Prue felt bad about what had happened. But they had done everything they could for this former partner. I say "former partner" because he was indeed a partner for years before alcohol destroyed his judgment and his life. Sometimes partners stop being partners. If that is the case, you don't have to stop acting like a partner. The rest of their employees saw how the owners had tried to help. (There are no secrets in small private companies.) The employees had always had a lot of respect for the couple, and this incident only served to underline it.

## SYSTEMIC THEFT

I also encountered theft in a completely different situation. This theft wasn't the result of one dysfunctional employee; it was systematic. And it required a different solution. But this story needs a little background.

My colleagues and I were working with a company then known as Zambia Consolidated Copper Mines Ltd., or ZCCM. The copper mines in the African nation of Zambia had been nationalized, and at the time, ZCCM was majority owned by the Zambian government. The company employed some fifty thousand people and provided about 95 percent of the country's hard currency.

But ZCCM was in trouble. Copper production was off. The mines were falling behind in deliveries to customers. Relations between management and labor—most of the workers were unionized—were contentious. The company's culture was hidebound and bureaucratic, mostly a legacy of an earlier incarnation under British management.

ZCCM's most immediate problem at the time was an acute lack of cash due to the falloff in production. As I walked through one of the mines, several thousand feet below ground, the miners confirmed this problem. (People don't lie in a mine, I was told. It's dangerous work. If you lie, you die.) The production decline, in turn, could be traced to a number of bottlenecks, specific obstacles that prevented the company from increasing output. The Mindola shaft, for example, was going to have to be shut down for sixty days so the company could take the steel-work to the next level down. But each day of lost production represented sixty tonnes of unmined copper and, consequently, lost cash.

ZCCM's chief operating officer, a man named Pius Maambo, liked the philosophy my colleagues and I were espousing: when you bring the economics of a business to life, the employees will respond with extra effort and fresh ideas, particularly if they share in the incremental profits that result. That's how we wound up in Zambia, wondering whether all those unionized mine workers could be persuaded to think and act like capitalists. Like partners.

So we developed what we called the cash bottleneck game:

1. Identify bottlenecks (we found five initial bottlenecks at ZCCM).
2. Meet with employees and management to get input on issues from their perspectives.
3. Examine the actual performance data versus what was budgeted for the past year.
4. Determine the additional cash generated by incremental improve-ment.
5. Develop an incentive for the employees involved, funded by 5–10 percent of the cash generated.
6. Roll out the "game" to the employees involved.
7. Track results, with updates at least weekly and communicated to everybody.
8. Celebrate successes, learn from results, and pay out incentives, typically over two to four months.

The results were astonishingly positive. The Mindola Redeep Shaft project was a good example. The game was to see whether the 205-member team could get the mine back up and running in less than the scheduled sixty days. Each day shaved off the schedule would result in an additional three days of pay for every team member. Mine managers felt there was little chance of finishing early but were willing to try.

As it happened, people busted their butts. They pitched in to help one another. They came up with new ideas. And in the end, they finished fifteen days early, a week before Christmas. So Pius, the COO, handed out the bonus payments to the entire team, with a congratulatory handshake. The crew had had no accidents, and the start-up of the mine went off without a hitch.

In the first nine months, the combined results of the initial five bottleneck games generated more than $10 million in additional cash, net of bonuses paid and our consulting fees. Management and employee trust soared, as did productivity and morale. And the accident rate fell, a major achievement.

To me, this was a model of what might be called partnership capitalism. Employees were learning to think like businesspeople. They were learning where their paychecks came from—and how to make those paychecks bigger. They earned an improved standard of living. Their customers benefited from the additional copper being produced.

When we Americans look at the developing world, we typically see crushing poverty and corrupt governments. The suggested solutions usually involve some kind of charity, as though these countries were hopeless and should be treated like helpless children. But people everywhere are better off when they earn their keep. Few will turn down a handout, but when the money is gone, nothing remains. Partnership capitalism gives everyone an opportunity, and the lessons learned provide perpetual benefits. If richer nations sincerely want to help the developing world, I think this is a vastly superior approach.

But—there's always a "but," isn't there?—ZCCM had some internal challenges. There was one manager in particular who caused problems. He was the head of the company's internal transport unit, and he was resisting the whole initiative. I asked him why he felt the ideas of economic engagement wouldn't work in his department.

"You don't understand, coming from the US," said the transport manager. "All my truck drivers are thieves."

"What do they steal?" I asked.

"Almost anything," he said. "Oil, gas, tires, batteries, you name it."

The manager and I examined the unit's financials and estimated the costs of theft. It was almost twice what the truck drivers were being paid.

"So here's an idea," I said. "A team bonus plan funded by reduction in theft."

"Nah," replied the manager. He told me the drivers would never go for it since they were making more by stealing. I told him he was nuts. At best they were getting ten cents on the dollar for sales to the black market, not to mention the personal risk. And there was no question that the honest truck drivers knew who the thieves were, even if they weren't stealing. Anyone who continued to steal would be stealing from themselves and the other drivers. Finally the manager agreed. I returned home to Kentucky.

Six weeks later, I was back. I paid a visit to the manager, only to find he had done nothing. I got up, closed the door to the manager's office, and said something like this:

"Listen. I think of myself as a reasonably ethical guy. But if I left home each morning, leaving my extended family of twenty behind, and saw that my young daughter was hungry again, you know what I would do? Anything. Anything at all. If that involved stealing, so be it.

"Now, we discussed a way where your truck drivers could actually earn more than what they earn by stealing, and you would cut your losses by seventy-five percent. Yet you have done nothing. So at this point you can do one of two things: initiate this program today, before I leave, or call the COO who hired me and try to get me fired." I picked up the phone and asked the man whether he should get the COO on the line. The manager decided to go with the first option.

Six months later, the company's costs for batteries, tires, fuel, and oil were a fraction of what they had been. The employees were taking home more money than ever, thanks to the bonus program. And the transport manager was fired for selling things on the black market.

Ironic, right?

It's all so simple. Leaders who assume that employees are all thieves will have employees who prove them right. Leaders who create an environment that fosters loyalty, teamwork, and honesty—and who share the rewards of those attributes—will have employees who respond accordingly. And if the economics are transparent, everyone tends to behave better. Thieves like the dark and hate the light. It's just one more way that economic engagement—and taking the high road—works.

## A DIFFICULT UNION—AND AN EVEN MORE DIFFICULT MANAGEMENT

I told the story of a unionized company in Australia, BHP, in the first chapter of this book. That story ended happily. Another engagement with a unionized company, here in the US, did not end happily. And it wasn't the union's fault.

It started with a call from the head of HR at Otis Elevator. Otis is a storied company, a leader in its industry. It was acquired by United Technologies Corporation in 1976, and at the time we're talking about it was still a division of UTC. It was spun off as an independent company called Otis Worldwide Corporation later, in 2020.

Anyway, I was trained as an engineer and I liked the idea of working with a large manufacturing company not so different from my first post-college employer, Briggs & Stratton. The Otis plant was located just outside of Bloomington, Indiana, home of Indiana University. It had just over a thousand employees, the vast majority union members. In the years prior to my visit, sales had been weak. But recently demand had soared, and the plant was now having a tough time keeping up. It was getting a lot of pressure from its corporate parent to increase production.

I knew that production capacity in a large, integrated plant like this one was determined by whichever department or process was the bottleneck. So I suggested we identify the bottleneck and start work there. The identification didn't take long because the plant manager spoke up immediately. "Our bottleneck is department four oh three," he said. "That's where we make the large telescopic cylinders that are the heart of many of our elevators." We agreed to start work in department 403, though I did have a concern that the relationship with the union—pretty poor in general—was particularly bad in department 403.

I suggested we hold a meeting with the plant and union leaders associated with department 403. The manager agreed. We met in a small auditorium on site. The HR head provided me with a brief introduction. I explained that my focus was on improving business results and the lives of the employees that drive those results. I can't say I generated much enthusiasm. But everyone agreed to go ahead with the first step, which was gathering information.

We gathered anonymous survey information from all shifts of department 403. We got similar data from the unit's management. We looked at customer input. We scrutinized production output and costs by month for the previous three years. Here's what all this data showed:

- Output varied widely during that three-year period, largely as a result of fluctuating demand.
- Overtime pay was consistently about 20 percent of total pay over this period, even when demand was soft.
- Recently, management had become desperate for more output. It had begun to contract out the manufacture of cylinders to a smaller competitor, at a modest cost premium.
- Management and union did not trust one another, and in some cases hated one another.

As planned, we reconvened the same group to go over the results. I started by mentioning that 20 percent of the cylinders were now being produced by the outside contractor. "They are exporting our jobs!" a union member yelled.

"Well, yes, they are," I said.

"You tell 'em, Bill," another union guy said. "I get it, though. The management is under a lot of pressure from corporate to improve the plant financials."

"You guys in the union clearly know how to manage the financials," I said. "I understand why you would be running twenty percent overtime at peak demand, but I see you have managed to get twenty percent overtime regardless of demand."

"You tell 'em, Bill," the finance manager said. The union reps were quiet.

I said, "Look, guys, I'm not on anyone's side. And it's pretty clear you guys don't like one another. But I see something you have in common. Both union job security and management job security would go up if elevator production increased, specifically in department four oh three. So I suggest that is what we should focus on. And if we are successful, the incremental production will not only improve everyone job security, it can also fund a bonus. Are we agreed?"

There was lots of muffled talk. Growing impatient, I said, "If you are opposed to moving in this direction, speak up."

No one did. Pretty soon, people started standing up to leave. I asked all of the union leaders to stay, along with any manager who wanted to.

After everyone else had cleared, I addressed the union leaders. "Look, I figure you know how to increase production. And I know what you think of your management, but it's you who are in control. So I suggest you get production up, starting next week.

"Admittedly, it will take us a couple weeks to come up with an incentive plan, which I will spearhead, working with management. If management does not finalize an incentive plan by then, you can stand proud, having called their bluff. And if they do, you'll have the extra money."

They seemed to like the sound of that.

Over the next two weeks, I did work with management on an incentive plan. Fortunately, the managers had excellent production information. They explained that some telescopic cylinders were much larger or more complex than others, so we had to take that into account. We developed a metric we called "weighted production," which we could examine every day. Two weeks after the group meeting, we looked at the data.

Even though we hadn't yet announced any bonus plan, production had already increased by more than 13 percent.

For the first time in my life, I suggested a retrospective bonus plan. I told management, "Yes, this is a little unconventional. But it's pretty clear the union team in department four oh three had already started playing. I think the right thing to do is to start the incentive plan from that point."

They agreed.

With an incentive plan in place, my next step was to speak with the union. As I was going through the scoreboard and the incentive plan, I explained that the management team had agreed to make the incentive plan start from two weeks ago. "They are doing something decent?" someone asked.

"Yeah, I think so," I replied, "and if we keep this up, it will mean roughly two hundred dollars in bonus pay for every member of department four oh three." At that point the union balked, saying that they wanted every union member in the plant to participate in the bonus. "It's all of us or none of us."

I promised to discuss that with management, but I have to say I wasn't on board with the idea. What had the other union members done to earn the extra money? As I thought it over, however, I asked myself a question: Which would be more motivating, getting an extra $200 in your own pocket or being responsible for putting twenty dollars in the pocket of every union member? The more I thought about it, the more I liked it. For sure, other departments and other union members would be cheering for department 403. And the opportunity to spread this concept to other areas of the plant would be enhanced.

Predictably, when I shared the union bonus demand with management, they screamed "socialism." I told them I had the same initial reaction, but I also discussed the potential benefits, not the least of which would be taking the union's advice. Management finally agreed. For the first time in years, they and the union were on the same page, working together toward a common goal. They followed the seventh principle:

### PARTNERSHIP PRINCIPLE #7

Partners always take the high road, putting people and collaboration first.

Unfortunately, this story does not end happily. Several weeks later, a new plant manager came on board. Within weeks he had fired the HR person and gotten rid of the "free-ride incentive plan for doing what the union should have done all along." When I asked to speak with him, he did not return my calls.

Four years later, I saw an announcement in the Bloomington paper: "Otis Elevator to Close Plant in Indiana." More than a thousand families whose lives revolved around employment at Otis would be affected.

So there was no win for the union. There was no win for Bloomington management. There was no win for UTC stockholders. There was no win for Otis customers. I am left thinking about what might have been and hoping that the new plant manager went down with the ship he sank.

# 8

# THE REAL MEANING OF PARTNERSHIP

**PARTNERSHIP IS A** way of running a company. It's a way of working together. But it's more than that: it's also a path to a better future. If you can **sustain** partnership, and if you can **extend** partnership, you will be helping create a better form of capitalism—capitalism that includes rather than excludes people and that is based on good profits rather than bad profits. Let me explain each of these elements.

## SUSTAINING PARTNERSHIP

If you've been around the business world for a while, you have probably noticed a sad fact. Many companies that seem to be great—well-managed, successful, desirable places to work, good people to do business with—don't survive the departure of the founder or CEO who made them that way.

You can see this phenomenon on a grand scale in James O'Toole's book *The Enlightened Capitalists*. O'Toole is a well-known expert in business and workplace management. He was a professor for many years at the Marshall School of Business, University of Southern California, and is founding director of the Neely Center for Ethical Leadership and Decision Making. He has written nineteen books, including *The Enlightened Capitalists*, which he says took him "tens of years" to produce. There's reason to believe he knows what he's talking about.

*The Enlightened Capitalists* tells the story of the many legendary business leaders who tried to create companies that worked for everyone—employees and customers and communities as well as shareholders. The list includes J. C. Penney, Milton Hershey, Ken Iverson of Nucor, Max De Pree of Herman Miller, and many others. But the book's subtitle is instructive: "Cautionary Tales of Business Pioneers Who Tried to Do Well by Doing Good." And the stories O'Toole tells bear out the caution. Nearly all of these leaders succeeded in creating admirable companies—for a while. But then something happened. They grew older. Some died before they could realize their vision. Others were distracted by different ventures or by the privileges of great wealth. When their attention waned, so too did their attempts to remake capitalism. In nearly every case, the companies they created are now quite ordinary. Some are still successful, others less so, but only a few are enterprises that anyone would hold up as exemplars.

We have described examples with similar outcomes in this book, albeit on a smaller scale. A leader gets excited about the principles of partnership and economic engagement. The company or corporate division that adopts these principles begins to thrive. Then a new leader comes in, as at Ameritech or Otis, and gets rid of the whole approach. Things go back to "normal." But normal, at least in those two cases, may be a toxic environment that contributes to the company's demise.

Let's look at this dilemma through the lens of Jim Collins and Jerry Porras. In their influential book *Built to Last* (HarperBusiness, 2004) they write:

Imagine you met a remarkable person who could look at the sun or stars at any time of day or night and state the exact time and date: "It's April 23, 1401, 2:36 A.M., and 12 seconds." This person would be an amazing time teller, and we'd probably revere that person for the ability to tell time. But wouldn't that person be even more amazing if, instead of telling the time, he or she *built a clock* that could tell the time forever, even after he or she was dead and gone?

The authors go on to explore the concept of clock building. Before the American Revolution, they note, political thought focused on how good the person at the top was. "If you had a good king, you had a good kingdom," and vice versa. The American founding fathers took a different approach. They didn't just ask who would be the best king or the best president. Instead, the founders of the country concentrated on such questions as "What processes can we create that will give us good presidents long after we're dead and gone?" "What type of enduring country do we want to build?" "On what principles?" "How should it operate?" "What guidelines and mechanisms should we construct that will give us the kind of country we envision?"

The system they created—elections, representation, checks and balances, and so on—is a kind of clockwork mechanism. It's imperfect, sure. But it survives. It was not dependent on any one individual. And whatever the bumps along the road, it's still holding together more than two centuries later.

The system I have outlined in this book is a clockwork mechanism for building a company of trusted partners—people who are engaged in the fundamental economics of the business and who share in the wealth that the business is creating. The goal is simple: to improve business results and the lives of the people who produce those results. To me, that is capitalism at its best. And if you do it right, it should endure long enough to create a better future.

Let's review both the mechanics—the elements of the mechanism—and the underlying ideas that inform them. The first step is finding your key number. That's the metric that will tell you whether you are winning or losing at business—whether you are creating a company that will be successful over the long haul or not. The idea here is to find a metric that everyone can understand and help improve. It has to be pretty simple because most people aren't accountants. But it also has to be directly related to the company's fundamental economics. "Quality" or "on-time delivery" or any other operational metric isn't sufficient unless it is somehow linked directly to business performance.

Remember, how you determine the key number is as important as the number itself. If you want employees to become trusted partners, you have to treat them like trusted partners. That means asking for their views and listening to their ideas, right from the beginning. Remember, too, that the goal here is to help people learn to think like owners. That means helping them understand the economics of the business so that they can make good decisions. It takes time for people to learn to think like an owner, and so it takes time for them to become trusted partners. The key number is one critical step on that path of learning. Also keep in mind that the key number tends to evolve as the issues facing the company evolve. It's wise to reassess it as part of your annual business planning process.

The second step is creating a scoreboard to track the key number, and then meeting weekly to review performance. This isn't a decision-making or problem-solving meeting. Its goal is to assess how *we* are doing right now and to gauge what's coming down the pike. You use the meeting to gather information about what has happened during the past week and what is likely to happen in the next few weeks. So you not only review your performance and compare it to budget; you also forecast results. Most companies I work with get pretty good at forecasting out at least three months. The process helps all the employees become progressively smarter about their business and consequently more in control of their future.

The key number and the scoreboard provide a guide for improvement initiatives. As we discussed, these can be part of a formal continuous-improvement system. Or they can come from informal sessions for proposing and then implementing ideas. This is where your partners get engaged with the economics of the business. They can see the effects of their actions on the company's performance. This reinforces—and adds to—the learning. Partners come to understand the effects of their actions. They can see what works and what doesn't.

Then comes sharing the wealth that you and your partners help create. An incentive plan tied to results is the simplest and most effective means for sharing the wealth in the short term. It motivates people to improve results. And it shows them that the company's owners are putting their money where their mouths are. Sometimes you can get away without an incentive plan, as we did at Capital One; the company was unable to provide a bonus, but individuals shared their success stories and that turned out to be pretty motivating all by itself. And sometimes the company is not profitable enough to pay any cash bonus, in which case the "bonus" for employees is greater job security. But I always encourage my clients to develop a cash payout whenever possible. It feels fair because it is fair, and it makes the whole thing more real. Over the long term, I advocate profit sharing of some sort and, where it makes sense, equity ownership through an employee stock ownership plan or some other mechanism. Ownership is really what turns employees into capitalists, so long as they also understand the economics of the business and have a chance to act on that understanding. Our country needs more capitalists, not fewer.

Please note something about this whole methodology. There's no mention of a charismatic leader. It doesn't require a larger-than-life CEO, someone who just naturally inspires people to go the extra mile. That's why I call it a clockwork mechanism—it works in ordinary companies staffed by ordinary people. Of course, it does require something that is sometimes in short supply in business: an initial willingness to trust one another, to listen to each other, and to work together. From there, the partnership principles build mutual trust and respect over time. But you can't even get started unless people are willing to give up whatever toxic combination of mistrust and cynicism they may be holding in their hearts. And you can't get started if the person in charge—the owner or CEO or division manager—won't give up the old, shopworn command-and-control approach to running a business. Fortunately, as it becomes clear that trusted-partner principles yield superior business results, interest among business owners continues to grow. Even private equity investors, such as the global investment firm KKR, are moving in this direction as they look for better results.

## EXTENDING PARTNERSHIP

This book has been about businesses and their employees. Its goal is to help companies redefine their relationship to the people on the payroll—to treat them as trusted partners and to get them economically engaged in the business through the implementation of eight Partnership Principles. (For a complete list, see the appendix.)

But to paraphrase John Donne, no company is an island. It is dependent on good relationships with its customers and its suppliers. It resides in a particular community, and its actions affect people in that community. A company can treat any or all of these stakeholders as partners, and doing so will likely help its business a great deal. When you do so, it builds trust. It allows you to solve common problems together. A company's business is no longer a struggle with its customers and suppliers to see who comes out on top. Instead, it is a collaborative effort.

Let me give you an example from my own experience.

Wellman, located in South Carolina, is a unique company in many ways. It is the largest employer in the small town of Johnsonville, employing 2,500 workers at its peak. The company has a patented process for recycling the nylon from used carpet that would otherwise end up in a landfill. The recycled nylon becomes nylon pellets that are used in injection molding machines. One common application is the manufacture of automotive parts, such as intake manifolds.

Most nylon is made from petroleum. A few years back, oil prices were rising. This fact, plus a growing interest in recycling, made the fundamentals of Wellman's business very attractive. But Wellman, as my brother Bob discovered one day, was in bankruptcy. Bob's career was fixing troubled companies. Working with the private equity company J. H. Whitney, he had already led several successful turnarounds. Wellman would be the largest one he had tackled to date. In 2008, he and Whitney purchased Wellman out of bankruptcy for just under $20 million.

The biggest problem, Bob felt, was the company's management. He called and asked for my help. I had some time available in my coaching business, so I took on Wellman as a client. I focused on sales and marketing, while Bob concentrated on plant operations. I found that the sales team, based in Detroit, seemed to have no common focus or direction that was consistent with the company's strengths. The situation was so bad that one of the sales staff, paid on salary, was spending most of his time selling for the competition. We fired him. It became clear that the sales managers had to be replaced.

With that, I agreed to become VP of sales and marketing, scaling back my coaching business for a while. Bob was still carrying most of the load at the plant. It took some time, but pretty soon costs began to drop and the plant's output began to increase. In fact, production increased so much that we needed to find more carpet to recycle. Overall, we were only capturing 3–5 percent of the total volume of used carpet. Most was still going into landfills.

Our supplier, however, had a distribution problem. That company was not set up to double or triple its volume. So Bob began working with the company as a partner. He explained Wellman's need for substantially increased volume. The supplier was well connected with the carpet companies, but it was not well capitalized. Bob suggested that he could set up distribution centers so the supplier could focus on getting the used carpet from the homes and offices to the local distribution center. Wellman would build and staff the distribution centers, taking care of getting the product to Johnsonville. In other words, both companies would play to their strengths. The plan worked, and before long we had all the used carpet we needed.

Now that we had more capacity, the bottleneck was sales. Could we increase customer demand to match our increased capacity? It was Bob's turn to put the heat on me. Getting approvals from the big automotive companies, especially Ford, was taking years. But I had an idea. Just as we partnered with our carpet supplier, I suggested we partner with Ford. At that time, we were heading into the annual strategic planning process we had instituted. So we asked Ford to participate in our strategy meetings, in person, providing us with an unfiltered "voice of the customer." And since it was quite a trip from Ford's headquarters in

Detroit to Johnsonville, we suggested we start by giving them a complete tour of our six-hundred-acre campus.

Ford accepted, telling us they would be bringing a team of engineering, quality, and purchasing staff. We let our operations team know that we would be showcasing Wellman's capabilities to our most important customer. They did a great job preparing, and the day went well. Many of the Ford representatives had never been to our facility. They had no idea of the scale of our operation, our quality procedures, or our technical capabilities. At the strategy meeting that afternoon, the Ford people did their own great job. They spelled out their priorities, described what they wanted to see from suppliers in general, and specified what they were most interested in, particularly as it related to our flagship product.

At the end of the meeting, the head of the Ford team rose to speak. He said, "I have been working at Ford for more than twenty-five years. I have never had one of our suppliers invite us to participate directly in their strategic planning meeting. Your level of candor and openness are impressive. My sincerest compliments to the Wellman team. We need to be doing more business with partners like this."

Needless to say, everyone at Wellman was thrilled. And the attention we started getting from Ford—quality advice, engineering part approvals, and long-term contracts—soared. Five years later, the company Bob and J. H. Whitney had purchased for just under $20 million was sold for more than $113 million. Every employee at Wellman benefited from the sale, as they were our internal partners. Bob just felt that was the right thing to do. Our supplier and customer partners also benefited. We could not have done this without them.

## A BETTER KIND OF CAPITALISM

I began this book talking about capitalism and socialism. I confessed to being a capitalist through and through. But I hope I was pretty clear about capitalism's chief shortcoming: the fact that it excludes so many. Too many Americans—too many people everywhere—don't understand business. They don't trust it. They figure that businesspeople are just out for themselves and don't mind screwing everybody else. These attitudes are widespread, and no wonder. Most people never get a chance to take part in business except by working for a wage or salary and doing as they are told.

How can we change this state of affairs? Obviously, individual businesspeople have to hold themselves to a high ethical standard. The more connivers and cheats there are in the business world, the more people who focus on short-term gain alone, the more everyone else will be convinced that all of business is corrupt. Long-term success in business or in life can't be built on a foundation of fraud. But it's equally important to transform the workplace so that people at every level of an organization get a chance to understand and to participate in the business. To learn the ropes. To become economically engaged. To become trusted partners and be treated as such. When a company transforms itself in this direction, good things happen. Its performance improves. It generates wealth for everybody. It turns hired hands into businesspeople—into capitalists. There's another effect as well: the company also has to hold itself to a high ethical standard. A partnership company is transparent, and transparency is always and everywhere the enemy of wrongdoing. In my view, that's how business becomes a true force for good. It's how businesspeople can be encouraged to take the high road and be rewarded for doing so.

But there's more to it than transparency and honesty. Your business has to add value to the world. It has to make good profits, not bad ones.

Businesspeople take the need for profit for granted. It's the lifeblood of any company—indeed, the lifeblood of capitalism. In a business, profit is an indicator of financial stability and success. It demonstrates that a company is serving customers efficiently and effectively. Companies that don't earn healthy profits over the long term don't stay in business. In a society, profitable companies make for a healthy economy, one that creates jobs and provides the goods and services that people need.

Many people, of course—and not just those who think of themselves as socialists—view profit as a dirty word. If a business is making a profit, so these people's thinking runs, it must be exploiting its employees or bilking its customers. Probably both. Unfortunately, some businesses provide these skeptics with evidence for their assertions. They really do bilk their customers and take advantage of their employees.

So there are good profits and bad profits, as the author Fred Reichheld of Bain & Company has repeatedly pointed out in his writings. Reichheld is primarily concerned with how companies treat their customers, so he defines bad profits as "profits earned at the expense of customer relationships":

> Whenever a customer feels misled, mistreated, ignored, or coerced, profits from that customer are bad. Bad profits come from unfair or misleading pricing. Bad profits arise when companies shortchange customers . . . by delivering a lousy experience. Bad profits are about extracting value from customers, not creating value. When sales reps push overpriced or inappropriate products onto trusting customers, the reps are generating bad profits. When complex pricing schemes dupe customers into paying more than necessary to meet their needs, those pricing schemes are contributing to bad profits.[21]

It's not hard to expand this definition a bit. Bad profits are also profits earned at the expense of a company's employees. They're profits earned by underpaying or mistreating the people who work for you, or exposing them to danger. Bad profits are profits earned at the expense of the community; for instance, by polluting the air or by figuring out some barely legal tax dodge. Bad profits inevitably focus on near-term benefits at the expense of longer-term success. So bad profits damage the longer-term value of the company and therefore hurt long-term shareholders. They give both profit and capitalism a bad name.

Reichheld's definition of good profits is equally useful and expandable:

> If bad profits are earned at the expense of customers, good profits are earned with customers' enthusiastic cooperation. A company earns good profits when it so delights its customers that they willingly come back for more—and not only that, they tell their friends and colleagues to do business with the company. . . . The right goal for a company that wants to break the addiction to bad profits is to build relationships of such high quality that those relationships create promoters, generate good profits, and fuel growth.[22]

From an employee's point of view, good profits are those that fund good working conditions, living wages, decent benefits, and an opportunity to share in the wealth. Good profits ensure job security and open up new opportunities for learning. From the community's point of view, good profits are those that allow a company to pay its taxes, maintain and improve its property, and generally act as a good corporate citizen. Over the long term, good profits add to everyone's wealth. These are the profits that fuel a better form of capitalism.

So let's sum this all up in the eighth and last partnership principle:

**PARTNERSHIP PRINCIPLE #8**

Partners work to build a better future.

If you build a company of trusted partners—if you foster economic engagement and learning, and if you share the wealth accordingly—you will almost certainly be building a company that generates and thrives on good profits. You will be creating a business that can thrive in all kinds of conditions and that will be a force for good. You will be making the world a better place.

I hope this book helps you along that path. Godspeed.

# APPENDIX

## The Partnership Principles—A Summary

1.  Partners know their business. They understand the economics.
2.  Partners have a clear goal. They know whether the business is winning or losing.
3.  Partners take responsibility for improvement. They value different points of view, and they hold each other accountable for results.
4.  Partners get a cut of the wealth they help create—and have a say in how big that cut is.
5.  Partners think long term, like owners.
6.  Partners face adversity together.
7.  Partners always take the high road, putting integrity and collaboration first.
8.  Partners work to build a better future.

# ENDNOTES

1. *Historical Statistics of the United States, Colonial Times to 1970* (US Department of Commerce, 1975), vol. 1, p. 179.

2. "Socialist Party Votes by Counties and States," University of Washington "Mapping America's Social Movements" project, accessed December 11, 2020, https://depts. washington.edu/moves/SP_map-votes.shtml.

3. "4 Factors Driving Record-High Employee Engagement in U.S.," Gallup website, posted February 4, 2020, accessed December 11, 2020, https://www.gallup.com/workplace/284180/factors-driving-record-high-employee-engagement.aspx. See also: "Historic Drop in Employee Engagement Follows Record Rise," Gallup website, posted July 2, 2020, accessed December 11, 2020, https://www.gallup.com/workplace/313313/historic-drop-employee-engagement-follows-record-rise.aspx.

4. "4 Factors Driving Record-High Employee Engagement in U.S."

5. "For most U.S. workers, real wages have barely budged in decades," Pew Research Center, posted August 7, 2018, accessed December 11, 2020, https://www.pewresearch.org/fact-tank/2018/08/07/for-most-us-workers-real-wages-have-barely-budged-for-decades/.

6. See stock-value calculator in Money Chimp's "Investing 101" program, accessed December 11, 2020, http://www.moneychimp.com/features/market_cagr.htm.

7. "Federal Reserve Board issues Report on the Economic Well-Being of U.S. Households," posted May 22, 2018, accessed December 11, 2020, https://www.federalreserve.gov/newsevents/pressreleases/other20180522a.htm.

8. "RETIREMENT SECURITY Most Households Approaching Retirement Have Low Savings," United States Government Accountability Office, posted May 2015, accessed December 11, 2020, https://www.gao.gov/assets/680/670153.pdf.

9. "The Economy Is Strong. So Why Do So Many Americans Still Feel at Risk?" *New York Times*, posted May 21, 2019, accessed December 11, 2020, https://www.nytimes.com/2019/05/21/opinion/trump-economy.html.

10. "Democrats More Positive About Socialism Than Capitalism," Gallup website, posted August 13, 2018, accessed December 11, 2020, https://news.gallup.com/poll/240725/democrats-positive-socialism-capitalism.aspx.

11. "Dealbook Briefing: Capitalists Fear a Socialist Revolt," *New York Times*, posted May 2, 2019, accessed December 11, 2020, https://www.nytimes.com/2019/05/02/business/dealbook/capitalism-socialism.html.

12. "Management Tools and Trends," Bain & Company website, posted April 5, 2018, accessed December 11, 2020, https://www.bain.com/insights/management-tools-and-trends-2017/.

13. "Walmart Touts New Staffing Model," *Arkansas Democrat-Gazette*, posted September 26, 2020, accessed December 11, 2020, https://www.arkansasonline.com/news/2020/sep/26/walmart-touts-new-staffing-model/.

14. *New American Standard Bible*, Mark 4:25.

15. An earlier version of this story appeared in Bill Fotsch and John Case, "Changing Workforce? Change the Way You Run Your Business," *Manufacturing Leadership Journal*, June 2016, pp. 59–63.

16. See James O'Toole's fine book *The Enlightened Capitalists* (HarperBusiness, 2019) for more detail on these and other profit-sharing pioneers.

17. O'Toole, p. 102.

18. Bo Burlingham, *Finish Big: How Great Entrepreneurs Exit Their Companies on Top* (Portfolio, 2013).

19. "Remember That Company With the $70K Minimum Wage? 5 Years On, the Results Suggest More Businesses Should Follow Suit," Inc. website, posted March 9, 2020, accessed December 11, 2020, https://www.inc.com/jessica-stillman/remember-that-company-with-70k-minimum-wage-heres-how-its-doing-now.html.

20. "Instead of Laying Off 20 Percent of His Company, This CEO Made an Unusual Decision. It's a Lesson in Emotional Intelligence," Inc. website, posted April 1, 2020, accessed December 11, 2020, https://www.inc.com/justin-bariso/instead-of-laying-off-20-of-his-company-this-ceo-made-an-unusual-decision-its-a-lesson-in-emotional-intelligence.html.

21. Fred Reichheld with Rob Markey, *The Ultimate Question 2.0* (Harvard Business Review Press, 2011), p. 25.

22. Reichheld, *Ultimate Question 2.0*, pp. 31–32.

# ACKNOWLEDGMENTS

**MANY INDIVIDUALS AND** companies contributed to this book and its insights. First and foremost is my editor, partner, and friend, John Case. We have collaborated on many projects for over twenty years. In my estimation, John is the best writer on the subject, as can be seen in his two books, countless articles, and the writing in this book. Thank you, John. Thanks, too, to my colleague Natalie Disney, a talented editor and administrator who has been a critical part of our business for many years.

It was Jack Stack and the people at SRC who initially introduced me to the concept of employees as trusted partners; that was back in 1988, when we set up a joint venture between my company, J. I. Case, and SRC. My years working with SRC's Great Game of Business helped me develop the ideas in this book, and the people there were great colleagues. I wish Jack, the Great Game, and current leaders Rich Armstrong and Steve Baker all the best.

The first people who were willing to work with me as a coach were Chris and Charlie LaBarge of LaBarge Products in St. Louis. Looking back, I did not know much and so was quite slow in helping them, but things worked out very well. The first large company I coached was the Zambia Consolidated Copper Mine, fifty thousand miners in the African nation of Zambia. The COO, Pius Maambo, was a great partner.

We learned how important it was to apply the principles of economic engagement at a local level.

Having worked with more than four hundred companies, each of which was important to me, I know I will be overlooking many. I hope they understand. I have learned from all of them and am indebted to every one. But there are particular companies that stand out. I was humbled to hear that Southwest Airlines, arguably the best-managed company in the US, had an interest in my support. Captain Moose Millard collaborated with John and me on what became known as Plane Smart Business. The word "authentic" took on new meaning as I worked with SWA. A very different but equally important client is FA Engineering; an eight-person company in 2013, it is today a fifty-person firm with rapid growth. The owners, Richard, Jeff, and Jeremy, have been true partners with me as we managed the challenges of growth over the years.

Anthony Wilder Design/Build has been recognized as a leader in their industry. Led by Anthony and Liz and COO Mark, the company has demonstrated the power of these concepts in its profitable growth. Roger and Jim at Boardman demonstrated how welders could be engaged in the business, particularly when the focus was the margin dollars on each job, something everyone could readily relate to. Carlson Travel (now CWT), and Janet in particular, showed how focusing these efforts on three of the company's twenty-seven branches could effectively provide experiment and control, validating the power of economic engagement. My friends in Australia, David and Prue, in their challenging business Post Form Laminates, have demonstrated again that this is a concept whose value is not restricted to North America. They continue to set records in sales and profits despite a declining market. Prue's leadership in ongoing customer interviews, the basis for understanding the economics, has been incredibly effective. And last, but hardly least,

Angus and Eric at Adams + Beasley Associates have shown how an incredible family culture combined with economic engagement drives industry-leading results.

I would like to acknowledge Jim Collins for taking time with me to discuss economic engagement, or (as we used to call it) open-book management. It became clear that this managerial process was what Jim called a mechanism, a repeatable process that enabled companies to prosper over time despite leadership changes. I would also like to acknowledge Daniel Pink, likely the most entertaining management guru I know. When I asked him his perspective on open-book management, he replied, "Great concept, lousy title." I think he was right.

Harvard Business School has helped shape my perspective since I was a student in 1981 and more recently as the parent of two HBS graduates. Dean Nitin Nohria introduced me to Professor Dennis Campbell and subsequently to his research associate Iuliana Mogosanu. All have enhanced my critical thinking, have introduced me to kindred spirits, and remain open to complementary perspectives. I am very grateful for their time, insights, and support.

I'm grateful to Georgette Green and the team at Indigo River Publishing, including editor Deborah Froese, copy editor Regina Cornell, and designer Emma Grace. And I send a particular vote of thanks to my fellow Indigo River author Rick Gillis, who encouraged us along the way and even suggested the title to this book.

Finally, I would like to acknowledge my family, past and present. My great-grandfather was an ardent socialist. My grandfather was a successful capitalist. I learned over time that both were right. My parents taught by example that faith, family, and friends were a priority in all aspects of life, including work. That perspective permeates the trusted-partner perspective. I grew up as the oldest of eight children. Leadership, common interest, and collaboration were daily lessons. My best decision of all time was marrying my wife, Joy. Her support, and at times the way she has challenged me, keep me focused and humble. Lastly, my daughter and two sons are simply the best. They make me want to be the best father I can be, including learning how to lead others by example.

I hope this book is seen as a thank-you to all those who contributed, both those I have explicitly mentioned and the many I haven't.

# INDEX

# ABOUT THE AUTHORS

## The Author

Over the past twenty-five years, Bill Fotsch has helped more than four hundred companies boost employee engagement and increase profits. He has worked with industry majors such as Southwest Airlines, BHP, Harley-Davidson, Roadway Express, Carlson Wagonlit Travel (now CWT), Scottish Hydro Electric, and Capital One. He has also coached many small-to-medium-sized privately owned businesses.

In the initial years of his career, Bill gained experience in management, marketing, and consulting at organizations such as Briggs & Stratton, Bain & Company, Case International, and Litton Industrial Automation. Later, as head coach at Great Game of Business, he spent over two decades applying the principles of economic engagement to help companies deliver results through a highly motivated staff. He founded Open-Book Coaching in 2012 to continue the work on his own.

Bill holds a bachelor of science in mechanical engineering from Marquette University and an MBA from Harvard Business School, where he graduated as a Baker Scholar. This is his first book.

## The Collaborator

John Case is an internationally known writer on management and employee ownership. He is author of the classic works *Open-Book Management* (Harper) and *The Open-Book Experience: Lessons from Over 100 Companies Who Successfully Transformed Themselves* (Addison-Wesley). He has written for *Inc.*, *Harvard Business Review*, and many other magazines. He has collaborated on several other books, including the international best-seller *Financial Intelligence*, published by Harvard Business Review Press.

Articles written by Bill and John have appeared in *Harvard Business Review*, *Inc.*, *Forbes*, and several other publications and websites.